Praise

D1460619

This book is a very informative and passionate guide to all things cheese. The Cheese Lady, Svetlana, has a great enthusiasm for educating people and enjoying cheese as part of a balanced diet.

Tom Kitchin, Chef Proprietor at The Kitchin

A romance novel of a cheese book, Svetlana invites us on a personal journey of delight and reconciliation through her love affair with cheese. It's uplifting at a time when so many of us have a complicated relationship with the food we eat.

Joe Schneider, Stichelton Dairy - maker of Stichelton cheese

This is essential reading for anyone who already loves cheese and wants to learn how to savour and enjoy it even more. It's a handy how-to guide to eating cheese the European way - not as a guilty habit but as part of a healthy balanced diet that is good for the soul.

Todd Trethowan, Trethowan Brothers - makers of Pitchfork Cheddar and Gorwydd Caerphilly

Svetlana's honest insight into her journey with cheese as a healthy food stuff, career choice and passion is creatively curated throughout this book to inspire others to love and really enjoy great cheese.

Tracey Colley, Director, Academy of Cheese

Svetlana's book is the definitive guide to understanding and enjoying cheese. Her passion for cheese, and life, is infectious and you can almost taste the cheese as you read! The Cheese Connoisseur's Way really is five steps to cheese happiness and is all you need to develop and nurture a long, loving and balanced relationship with cheese.

Claire Blackler, Wine Educator, Founder of Case Studies Wine School

A passionate and personal paean of praise to milk-based protein. A reminder too that we should recognise, treasure and support the deep reservoirs of knowledge of folk like Svetlana in our midst.

Simon Briggs, Director, Great Grog Independent Wine Merchants

A very personal and approachable insight into specialist cheese. Svetlana successfully demystifies fine cheese, empowering the reader to make more conscious choices when buying and enjoying it.

Rachael Sills, Käseswiss, Natural Alpine cheese specialist

THE
CHEESE
CONNOISSEUR'S
HANDBOOK

HOW TO DEEPEN YOUR UNDERSTANDING &
ENJOYMENT OF FINE CHEESE YEAR-ROUND

SVETLANA KUKHARCHUK

Re think

First published in Great Britain in 2021
by Rethink Press (www.rethinkpress.com)

© Copyright Svetlana Kukharchuk

All rights reserved. No part of this publication may be reproduced, stored in or introduced into a retrieval system, or transmitted, in any form, or by any means (electronic, mechanical, photocopying, recording or otherwise) without the prior written permission of the publisher.

The right of Svetlana Kukharchuk to be identified as the author of this work has been asserted by her in accordance with the Copyright, Designs and Patents Act 1988.

This book is sold subject to the condition that it shall not, by way of trade or otherwise, be lent, resold, hired out, or otherwise circulated without the publisher's prior consent in any form of binding or cover other than that in which it is published and without a similar condition including this condition being imposed on the subsequent purchaser.

Cover image © Amanda Farnese Heath

Interior photography by Amanda Farnese Heath

To my family

Contents

Chapter 6

Chapter 7

Introduction

People call me the Cheese Lady. I'm the founder of The Cheese Lady shop, a specialist cheese shop offering a curated selection of complex farmhouse and artisan cheeses, also known as fine cheeses. My real speciality is finding the perfect cheese for each person's unique palate, favourite drink or occasion.

But if you think I am just about cheese, you may be missing the point. My purpose in this world is to show people how to *really* savour life and I believe that fine cheese is the perfect vehicle for that.

I've made it my mission to raise fine cheese awareness and appreciation and to transform the way British people eat cheese. As a nation we need to get rid of the guilt and stop the yo-yo eating habits. Instead, we should integrate fine cheese into our normal diet throughout the year, just as other Europeans do. I want to inspire you to believe that fine cheese is good for your body and soul and should be enjoyed guilt-free as part of your normal diet throughout the year.

My career in fine cheese spans fifteen years. I worked with the biggest specialist cheesemonger in New York City, Murray's Cheese, selling cheese in their flagship store in Greenwich Village and their Grand Central store to discerning and affluent foodies. I learned the art and science of traditional cheesemaking by hand-crafting a farmhouse cheese in Scotland and I published my first book on cheese in Russian in 2010. I have been a cheese judge at the Royal Highland Show and the World Cheese Awards and am accredited with the Academy of Cheese. In addition, I hold a Level 3 Wine and Spirits Education Trust (WSET) certificate, which qualifies me as a wine and spirits professional. I want to share my specialised knowledge of both fine cheese and fine beverages.

When I was younger, I was not a foodie. In my late teens and early twenties I battled with an eating disorder that made me feel isolated, obsessed with calorie counting and imprisoned in my mind. I have overcome the disease and discovered that it is possible to eat any natural food in balance - even cheese, chocolate and ice cream - and not gain weight. Today, not only do I get better nourishment, I also have a much more positive outlook on life.

I see many cheese lovers struggling with eating cheese guilt-free. They believe cheese is fattening and dangerous to their health. As a result, they cannot fully enjoy the object of their temptation. This creates a dilemma in every cheese lover's mind. How do you reconcile something so delicious with being so potentially bad for your health?

I am not a physician, nutritionist or psychologist, but having had my share of struggles with food and health and having found a sustainable diet solution, I like to share my experience to help others. In this book, you will discover how to include fine cheese into a balanced diet, especially since it has numerous health benefits. The only caveat is that you need to know how to tell quality cheese from the inferior versions, and how to enjoy it in beneficial amounts.

Despite the wider current movement towards natural and organic over highly processed and mass-produced food, cheese lovers still struggle to tell good cheese from bad. As a result, they end up stuck in the unhappy situation where they feel guilty for enjoying cheese and resort to restricting it in their diet and obsessing over calorie counting. What's even sadder is that they are missing out on living fully and really savouring life.

It doesn't have to be this way. Any natural food, especially farmhouse and artisan cheese, should be about enjoyment, wholesome nourishment and celebration.

This book is for you if you love real cheese and all its intricacies and complexities. If you start salivating just thinking of the nice gooey ones or the firm crunchy ones. If you love discovering regional specialities wherever you go and visiting as many specialist cheese shops as you can find. It is for food enthusiasts who take pleasure in exploring cuisines and flavours and who want foods made from natural and unadulterated ingredients known to have positive effects on health. If currently you buy your cheese exclusively from supermarkets but wish to broaden your taste horizons and take your cheese understanding to a whole new level, this book is definitely for you.

I want to demystify fine cheese and help you enjoy it fully and joyfully throughout your life and include it as part of a healthy balanced diet. By reading this book, you will evolve from an occasional cheese consumer who is a bit confused about the different varieties, and anxious about the health dangers of cheese, into a confident fine cheese connoisseur who enjoys cheese throughout the year and knows how to get more pleasure out of every bite. You will learn how to *savour your life.*

My method is called the Cheese Connoisseur's Way. It is the five steps to cheese happiness that will help transform the way you look at cheese, appreciate it and savour it. The book is divided into two parts - Understand and Savour - and each of the five steps fits neatly within these parts.

The five steps of the Cheese Connoisseur's Way are as follows:

Part One: Understand

△ Step 1: Developing cultured taste

△ Step 2: Seeking out curated service

Part Two: Savour

△ Step 3: Mastering continuous enjoyment

△ Step 4: Learning conscious appreciation

△ Step 5: Nourishing connection

At the end of each chapter you will find my 'spotlight on cheese'. These will focus on particular cheeses, giving you their history, how they are made, how best to use them and what wine or other drink to choose to accompany them. By going through the five steps of the Cheese Connoisseur's Way you will gain more clarity and confidence as a cheese consumer. You will be able to enjoy it consciously and continuously and with peace of mind when it comes to your health. You will learn about the virtues of fine cheese, which have positive effects on your physical and mental wellbeing. The joy and pleasure you will get from making the most out of every cheese experience will be sure to help you alleviate stress and improve the overall quality of your life.

PART ONE
UNDERSTAND

In Part One I am going to take you through the history of cheese, explain how cheese is produced and discuss the significant changes that have happened to traditional cheese in the post-industrial era. In Chapters 1 and 2 we will look at the different varieties of cheese and what makes some healthier than others. Then we will look at how to make great choices when shopping for cheese and how to find the ones that will be just perfect for your unique palate, drink of choice or occasion. In Chapters 3 and 4 we will take the first two steps of the Cheese Connoisseur's Way to cheese happiness so that by the time you have completed Part One you will have a basis for understanding cheese and all of its wonderful complexities.

CHAPTER 1

Sweet Dreams Are Made Of Cheese

For many people, delicious cheese is the stuff of dreams. At the same time, many cheese lovers struggle with moderation and a guilty conscience as a result of enjoying cheese. They are often confused about what 'good' or 'real' cheese is, how to find it and how to fit it into a healthy diet. In this chapter, I'd like to share my journey from being a cheese novice to a cheese aficionado for life. I'll introduce you to my model, the Cheese Connoisseur's Way, covering the five elements of cheese happiness I've developed over the years that will help you gain a clearer understanding of what good cheese is, where and how to buy it and how to enjoy every morsel in a healthy way.

To eat or not to eat?

During the years of talking cheese to people in my professional capacity, I have learned that a lot of people don't understand cheese very well. They do not see a clear difference between *industrial* cheese and *fine* cheese. As a result, they are scared of *all* cheese, when it comes to its potential health dangers. Due to this lack of understanding, people believe that all cheese is bad for their health, that it causes nightmares, makes them fat and is going to skyrocket their cholesterol. You name it, I've heard it all. They cannot enjoy it regularly, let alone without guilt.

While it is true that if you overindulge in cheese (or any other food), especially too close to bedtime, you may get disturbed sleep and even gain weight eventually, it is certainly not the direct result of enjoying good cheese in moderate amounts.

My fundamental belief in life is that *farmhouse* and *artisan* cheese is good for you and it can and should be enjoyed year-round. Not only is it known to have mood-lifting effects and therefore is good and necessary for our mental wellbeing, fine cheese is also a great source of nutrients and micronutrients such as protein, calcium and some important vitamins.

Then there is the issue of fat content, which puts some people off. According to the Organisation for Economic Co-operation and Development, many British people lead unhealthy lifestyles and 64% of adults are overweight or obese.[1] While it is clear that we do have a health crisis on our hands, the modern processed food diet is the cause of many health issues, as well as the current obesity crisis. Just think about it – cheese has been around for millennia, whereas cardiovascular diseases, obesity, depression and other mental health disorders became major health concerns only during the last century. This time also saw rapid changes in food production techniques, which include processing, as well as use of additives, pesticides and growth hormones. These changes have been implicated in

---

1   Organisation for Economic Co-operation and Development,
     'Health at a glance 2019: United Kingdom' (2019)

causing serious health problems.[2] On the other hand, foods that are sustainably produced and natural, additive free, nutrient rich and alive are good for you when consumed in moderation, *even if* they contain fat and naturally occurring sugars.[3]

My conclusion is that wholesome well-made cheese has a place in our diets, as long as you enjoy it in moderate amounts as part of a healthy varied diet but also with mindfulness and joy. Especially since it is becoming more apparent that *what* we eat and *how* we eat it can have profound effects on our physical and mental health.[4] To ensure our long-term wellbeing it is imperative that we choose our sources of nourishment wisely, as our energy levels, outlook on life and even longevity are directly influenced by our daily food choices. It is also essential that we enjoy these wholesome foods mindfully, in moderation and ideally in good company (although the absence of good company should not be a reason to scrap gastronomic pleasures). Food has a real power to heal, connect and transform not only our bodies, but also our minds and souls.

2   AF Luzzi & WPT James, 'European diet and public health: the continuing challenge', *Eurodiet* (2001)
3   A Mie et al, 'Human health implications of organic food and organic agriculture: a comprehensive review', *Environmental Health* (2017)
4   Mental Health Foundation, 'Feeding minds: the impact of food on mental health' (2007)

Origins of the Cheese Connoisseur's Way

As you'll learn later in this book, fine cheese is a perfect example of a wholesome food that is sustainably produced and natural, free of additives, rich in nutrients and alive. What we need to master is enjoying it *in balance* and *with joy*.

I cannot tell you how often I get asked about my secret of staying healthy and fit while working with cheese. I have come to realise that my philosophy on eating cheese can be paralleled to that of the French, Italian and Greek cultures and it is from this way of thinking that the Cheese Connoisseur's Way evolved. Through my extensive travel and self-education, I've discovered the beauties of other cultures, and especially the balance and wisdom of the Mediterranean diet. Our continental friends do not exclude cheese from their daily fare. Cheese is a normal part of their lives and has been for centuries. Hardly any lunch or dinner with friends or family goes by without a cheeseboard. By contrast, a lot of us Brits wait until Christmas or other festive periods to spoil ourselves with some dairy delights. Cheese has become a dietary outcast, believed to be detrimental to health. There needs to be a cultural shift when it comes to cheese appreciation in this country. We need to re-discover the pure wholesome kind of cheese. We need to fall in love with it all over again and keep enjoying it throughout our lives in balance and with joy.

Fundamental terms

To start our discussion on cheese quality and to initiate you into the world of fine cheese, I would like to introduce you to three fundamental terms that I will be using throughout the book. My area of expertise relates specifically to these varieties of cheese:

△ **Farmhouse cheese** is made in a traditional way, in which the key stages of the process are performed by a professional cheesemaker, and it is the product of one farm. That means that the milk for cheesemaking came from the same farm where the cheese was crafted.

△ **Artisan cheese** is made in a traditional way, in which the key stages of the process are performed by a professional cheesemaker, but the milk is sourced from nearby farm(s).

△ **Fine cheese** is shorthand for farmhouse and artisan cheese.

There are many other terms that can be used instead of fine cheese. For instance, real cheese and traditional cheese. Personally, I like the parallel between fine cheese and fine wine. Just like fine wine, fine cheese is made of outstanding quality ingredients by true masters of the craft and can have 'a taste of place', the concept known as *terroir* in the wine world.

With this book I would like to show you how to understand and fully appreciate fine cheese. The two fundamental parts of the Cheese Connoisseur's Way are Understand and

FIORE SARDO
Artisan ewe's milk cheese from Italy

Savour. They are designed to increase your understanding of cheese, dispel your fear of eating it and show you how to get more flavour and pleasure out of every morsel. The two main parts are further broken down into five elements that will take you from a cheese novice to a fine cheese connoisseur by showing you how to:

△ Develop a **cultured taste** - understand the different varieties of cheese and develop a discerning eye for cheese quality.

△ Seek out **curated service** - learn to purchase cheeses that are perfect for your unique palate, favourite drink or occasion.

△ Master **continuous enjoyment** - understand the nutritional composition of cheese, its health benefits and how to fit cheese into a healthy balanced diet year-round.

△ Learn **conscious appreciation** - learn how to get more out of every morsel of cheese and pair cheeses with wine.

△ Nourish **strong connections** - how to use cheese to strengthen your social connections and learn the cheeseboard fundamental.

Not only will you be able to enjoy delicious cheese year-round and get great pleasure from it, you'll also reap significant physical and mental health benefits. When you master all five concepts, you may also get to savour life more.

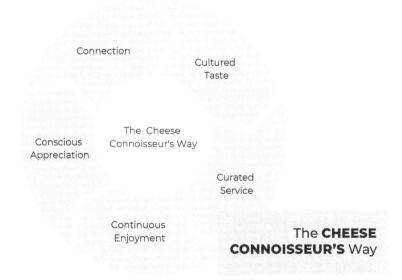

Connection

Cultured Taste

The Cheese Connoisseur's Way

Conscious Appreciation

Curated Service

Continuous Enjoyment

The **CHEESE CONNOISSEUR'S** Way

The journey to cheese

The Cheese Connoisseur's Way has developed through the experience I have gained in becoming the Cheese Lady. 'How do you manage to stay so slim? You work with cheese!' I hear people exclaim all the time when they meet me for the first time. A slim and healthy-looking cheese lady strikes most people as a contradiction in terms. People struggle to believe that someone can have cheese as often as their heart desires and remain within a healthy BMI range. I'd like to assure you that I'm not one of those people who is incredibly lucky to have superior genes that burn all the fat off the second I consume it. What I have is a system that I have developed that has taken me from being weight-obsessed, battling with an eating disorder, to someone who is completely comfortable and free to enjoy any food I desire, including cheese.

I grew up in Russia, in a culture where most women, desperate to look thin, were caught up in an endless cycle of bingeing and starving. Not surprisingly, I believed that any ounce of weight on my bones was unattractive and that you had to be slim to be beautiful. This outlook was ingrained into me and stayed with me for the majority of my teenage years. It resulted in an eating disorder and obsession with my looks and weight until I was given a stark wake-up call in my early twenties by an honest doctor who told me that I would die prematurely if I carried on the same way. This started my transformation and evolution to where I am today.

I immersed myself in studying nutrition. The newly gained knowledge gave me the power to make educated and better decisions. The main learning points were that food had to be natural, unadulterated and ideally not processed and had to be enjoyed in balance - not too much but not too little. This opened my eyes and made food choices much easier. Today I choose real natural foods, whereas anything marketed by McDonalds or similar businesses has no appeal to me. I have about as much desire to consume anything from the 'Golden Arches' as I do to eat my own shoe.

A few years after I started my nutritional transformation, I found myself living and working in one of the greatest cities in the world - New York City. Freshly out of university in Pennsylvania, I moved to New York to look for a 'proper job', which I thought was going to be in something to do with international relations (my major at university), but instead I fell in love with cheese.

This vibrant and continuously buzzing city seduced me with the outstanding quality of its food choices. Fresh hand-stretched steaming mozzarella? You got it! Crunchy artisan baguettes? No problem! Hand-crafted perfectly balanced chocolates? *Bien sûr!* Myriads of scrumptious farmhouse cheese? Absolutely. Needless to say, New York was the best place to be a foodie and go deep on any food my heart desired.

My first job was as a chocolate café deputy manager at the Saks Fifth Avenue department store. One day my boss thought I should learn more about chocolate at the Fancy Food Show, the biggest food show in the United States, and that's where I discovered fine cheese. Not cheese as I knew it from my childhood or even supermarkets in

Pennsylvania – rubbery and bland – but colourful, aromatic and lingering. I could not believe the variety of flavours, textures and aromas that came from something as simple as milk. I immediately wanted to know more.

After a quick Google search, I found a volunteering opportunity at Murray's Cheese, where I helped to prepare for cheese and wine events. At the time, Murray's retailed over 300 varieties of farmhouse and artisan cheese from around the world and thus appeared to me as the absolute best place to immerse oneself in cheese learning. I took a full-time job as a cheesemonger and started selling cheese to discerning foodies at the flagship Greenwich Village store and bustling Grand Central stall. To deepen my understanding of the whole cheesemaking process, I also completed Murray's affinage (cheese maturation) internship in their underground caves. After brushing, washing and plucking cheeses for hours I smelled like cheese myself. But I loved it! I gained incredible insights into the development and evolution of cheese as it matures, as well as some important know-how, tricks of the trade and industry contacts.

One of these contacts was Hervé Mons, who is one of the most acclaimed French cheese refiners. His speciality is going around France sourcing young farmhouse and artisan cheeses and maturing them to perfection in his cellars in Auvergne-Rhône-Alpes. I was lucky to be invited to spend some time there and learned a great deal from Hervé and his team about the art of affinage.

Of course, no one can fully understand the beauty and complexity of traditional cheese if they haven't made one with their own bare hands. I got a job as an assistant cheesemaker at a farm in Fife, Scotland, making a cow's milk Cheshire-style cheese called Anster, and began to appreciate the amazing work that professional cheese-makers do. I can still vividly remember my sore back from hanging over the vat wall piling cheese curds into moulds, followed by flipping the monstrous 20 kg wheels the next day.

I opened my first specialist cheese shop in St Andrews in 2010 and after selling it a few years later I opened my current shop in East Lothian, Scotland. Both shops were founded on a strong mission to champion farmhouse and artisan cheeses, but the second business also acquired an additional layer to its mission – to promote good health, balance and connection.

People often wonder why I gave up a career in international relations to sell cheese. My honest response is that I feel I can make a greater difference. Cheese is a perfect vehicle for slowing down, savouring life and connecting with our favourite people. Cheese makes us happier, and if the world is full of happy people, it is a good place to live. That is why I do what I do.

I also believe there is great synergy between good health, responsible consumption and production. Eating natural foods on their own is not enough because even natural foods can be overindulged in and can have negative effects on health. Ever since I recovered from my struggle with my eating disorder and depression, maintaining strong physical and mental wellbeing has been hugely important to me. I know that good health is not possible in a vacuum.

It is directly related to and influenced by what we eat and how we eat. Eating natural foods in balance, with joy and in good company is where the real power is. That's why I champion traditionally produced foods such as farmhouse and artisan cheese and a joyful eating culture.

The Cheese Connoisseur's Way is based on my philosophy on cheese and life and will help you evolve from a cheese beginner who is a bit confused by all the cheese jargon, feels concerned about the health implications of enjoying cheese and generally feels they could be missing out on the deliciousness of life, to a connoisseur with a deep understanding and appreciation of fine cheese and the knowledge of how to enjoy cheese throughout the year, not just at Christmas.

 Spotlight on cheese: GRUYÈRE

Gruyère AOP: a taste of Swiss history

When I'm asked what my favourite cheese is, I get stuck. They are all my 'babies' and I love them equally. But if I were asked what cheese I would take with me to a desert island, I would have to pick Gruyère. I never get tired of its perfectly smooth mouth-coating texture, complex nuanced taste and aroma, and heart-warming aftertaste. I love how versatile it is too, as it can shine on a cheeseboard and in cooking. It gets only better with age and never goes out of style. My customers often hear me calling this classic and timeless cheese the Chanel of the cheese world.

LE GRUYÈRE AOP
One of the most renowned and ancient
artisan cheeses from Switzerland

Gruyère has played a major part in Swiss cheese history. Its origin can be traced back to 1115. During the seventeenth century, the Gruyère name gained official recognition and started to be exported, but it was only in 2011 that it became legally protected by European law. Today there are many rules and regulations in place to ensure the high quality and authenticity of Gruyère, in particular in relation to the quality of the milk. Cows must be fed a primarily grass diet in the summer and hay in the winter, whereas fermented feeds like silage are banned. In the dairy, the quality of the vat used plays a central role. It must be made from copper as it is known to impart better flavour to cheese and strengthen its microelement composition.

Once the new wheels of Gruyère are produced, for three months they are looked after by the cheesemaker, who regularly washes them with a water and salt solution to help rind development. Then the cheeses are passed on to one of eleven professional affineurs who continue to mature the cheeses for many months to come.

All wheels are graded (in Switzerland, the grading process is called 'taxation') at five months old and those that fail the test can no longer be called Le Gruyère AOP. Many people think the most popular cheese of Switzerland is the famous large-eyed cheese called Emmentaler (also commonly known as Emmental). In fact, it is Gruyère, which unlike Emmentaler has no eyes (holes) and is famous for its smooth, dense paste and long, complex flavour.

How to enjoy Gruyère

There are four main varieties of Gruyère you can find on the market today:

- △ **Le Gruyère AOP:** matured for six to nine months, this is a semi-firm going on firm textured cheese with a buttery sweet taste. Great for everyday use in salads, sandwiches and cooking. This young Gruyère has a good melting capacity and can be used as a base for fondue. I recommend that you enhance it with the Reserve or Alpage varieties to add more depth and complexity.

- △ **Le Gruyère AOP Reserve:** matured for over ten months. This cheese is firm in texture with a long fruity and nutty flavour. Some Reserve Gruyères can be matured for significantly longer periods of time, and therefore will offer a greater complexity, depth of flavour and will shine on a cheeseboard. Reserve Gruyère is a wonderfully versatile cheese and can pair with white, red and sparkling wines. Use the age of the cheese as the guide to selecting the body of the wine but if in doubt ask for guidance from your cheesemonger.

△ **Le Gruyère AOP Bio:** this version is made with certified organic milk and can be six to nine months old or over ten months.

△ **Le Gruyère d'Alpage AOP:** this variety is produced only from mid-May until mid-October high up in the Alps where cows graze on the amazing Alpine flora. Seven days a week, cheesemakers turn fresh milk into cheese. The whole process is performed primarily by hand and takes place over an open fire. Gruyère d'Alpage is an experience to be savoured slowly with your finest bottle of red wine or champagne.

If you would like to deepen your understanding of this amazing cheese, I recommend visiting La Maison du Gruyère, located close to the medieval town of Gruyères that gives the Gruyère cheese its name. In this show dairy you can go on an interactive and informative tour that takes a look at the history and peculiarities of Gruyère, including the quality of its milk and the role of local flora in its quality. The culmination of the tour is viewing Gruyère being made live from the viewing platform, after which you can sample the finished product in the shop and indulge in a fabulous fondue in the restaurant at La Maison or in the town of Gruyères. This incredible Swiss cheese is a slice of history. I encourage you to take your time to savour it fully.

SUMMARY

In this chapter, we have looked at the dilemma most cheese lovers experience. We explored how fine cheese can fit into our eating culture and I briefly introduced you to the Cheese Connoisseur's Way, my five-element philosophy on cheese and life. I then told you about my journey to becoming the Cheese Lady.

With each new element introduced in the following chapters, you will progress from being a beginner in your understanding of cheese to enjoying it at its best with a deep appreciation and understanding of the quality you are consuming.

In the next chapter we will take a dive into the history of cheese and begin to understand some elements of cheesemaking.

CHAPTER 2

What Is Cheese?

These days, consumers find themselves confused and bombarded by contradictory information, especially when it comes to something seemingly as simple as cheese. Understanding is the fundamental first step in becoming an enlightened consumer. In this chapter, I cut through this confusion as I take you through the history of cheese and explore the fundamentals of how cheese is made.

An overview of cheese history

Primitive cheese

The importance of exploring the history of various foods in our society cannot be underestimated. Understanding the origin of foods as ancient as cheese helps us appreciate the role that it has played in our society for millennia. No one knows exactly when or where cheese was first made but it is thought to have coincided with the domestication of goats and sheep around 8,000 BC.[5] It was likely that people found that milk, when left in the sun or in a warm environment, naturally soured due to the action of lactic acid bacteria naturally present in milk. They drained the liquid that separated and the remaining mass became a primitive version of fresh cheese.

---

5   Kindstedt, P, *Cheese and Culture: A history of cheese and its place in the Western civilization* (Chelsea Green Publishing, 2012)

Some archaeologists name certain territories of modern-day Iraq, between the Tigris and Euphrates rivers, the cradle of civilisation. This is where they believe products like bread and cheese originated. Others believe that it happened in the ancient Egyptian and Sumerian territories. The geographical uncertainty is immaterial when it comes to understanding the importance of cheese invention in that era, when the survival of humans depended on receiving crucial nutrients from food, which was scarce.

The invention of rennet

The next revolutionary development in cheesemaking was the discovery of rennet, the ferment responsible for curdling milk and separating the solids, known as curds, from the liquids, known as whey. There is a wonderful legend about how it happened. Many centuries ago, a caravan of camels was crossing the desert, carrying with it merchants and their provisions. Back then, milk was transported in vessels made of dried lambs' stomachs. After hours of travel across the scorching desert, the merchants stopped to rest. They laid out their provisions and started to pour milk. But instead of white milk they found semi-clear liquid running out, and inside the vessel they found a white crumbly substance. The merchants did not hesitate and tried the newly discovered substance. This new food tasted good and also proved to be filling. It became apparent that the rennet present in lambs' stomachs caused the whey to separate from the curd and it improved the taste of the final product. During the centuries that followed, people continued to improve cheesemaking methods. They invented purposefully designed cheese moulds that allowed better whey drainage, and new techniques for moulding and pressing cheeses. Salt was introduced and was added to cheese to extend its shelf life.

Roman, Greek and medieval cheesemaking

The ancient Greeks and Romans made a huge contribution to improvements in cheesemaking techniques and to spreading cheese across Europe and beyond. Roman soldiers' daily rations always contained cheese. As a result, wherever a new Roman stronghold was established, cheesemaking practices followed. In the Middle Ages, a lot of cheeses were invented in monasteries, especially those where consumption of meat was prohibited. Monasteries were particularly good for certain styles of cheeses, such as the washed rind cheeses like Munster, Époisses de Bourgogne and Abbaye de Cîteaux. Some of these ancient cheeses have become extinct, but many are still produced to this day, and others have been brought back from extinction.

Industrialisation and wars

The twentieth century proved catastrophic for traditional cheesemaking. The devastation of two wars and the new industrial economy ruthlessly did away with farmhouse and artisanal cheesemakers. As a result, by the mid-twentieth century their numbers had sharply declined. The small farmhouse cheesemaking operations were replaced by huge creameries that produced tonnes of cheese a day. On the upside, industrially produced cheese provided basic nutrition to the starving population. On the downside, these cheeses noticeably lacked aroma intensity, depth and complexity of flavour. Moreover, they also lacked important nutrients, including fats, vitamins and minerals.

Traditional cheesemaking renaissance

Fortunately for us, traditional cheesemaking was not completely eradicated. In the 1970s the world started to experience a dynamic renaissance in traditional cheese-making practices. Leading this revival were France, Italy and Spain. The industrial economy giants, the UK and the USA, started to experience the same revival. Today, Britain boasts more cheeses by name than even France.[6]

Fundamental cheesemaking elements

Cheesemaking may appear to be a simple and straight-forward process, as it involves only a small number of fundamental steps and ingredients. To start you need just four ingredients - milk, starter culture, rennet and salt - to carry out the following steps:

1. Acidify milk (naturally or with starter cultures).

2. Add rennet to separate liquids (whey) from solids (curd).

3. Cut/stir the curd.

4. Drain the whey off.

---

6   Thomas, H, 'Whey to go: how British cheese is taking on the continent', Farmdrop blog (23 April 2019), www.farmdrop.com/blog/british-cheese-artisans-competing-continent, accessed April 2021

5. Add some salt (to most varieties of cheese).

6. Place the curds in forms.

7. Dry the wheels and mature them.

There is much more to this process than meets the eye. Small but significant tweaks and additional steps along the way account for the creation of different styles of cheese. For instance, the starting temperature of milk is responsible for favouring certain types of starter cultures that in turn lead to creating completely different styles of cheese. Mesophilic cultures, which are low temperature-loving cultures, will grow at 25-30°C and produce soft cheeses like Brie and Munster, whereas thermophilic cultures, which are high temperature-loving cultures, will grow best at 35-41°C and produce firm cheeses like Gruyère and Parmigiano Reggiano. Some recipes may call for additional steps such as cooking the curd and milling it, but these steps are not necessary for all cheese varieties.

There can also be noticeable variations in the quality of basic ingredients - milk and rennet, particularly - and attitudes to the cheesemaking process and maturation that lead to the creation of various grades of quality. Only the producers who are fully dedicated to making their milk shine and want to carry out every step to the highest standard produce the finest cheese. Inexpensive cheeses are cheap for a reason, which is that corners are cut all along the cheesemaking and refining process.

Rennet

Cheese containing rennet

Milk has to be curdled and the solids (curds) need to be separated from liquids (whey) to make cheese. The majority of cheeses produced today are made with rennet, an enzyme that helps to achieve just that by curdling the proteins present in milk and releasing whey from the curd. Traditional rennet comes from the stomach of nursing calves, kids or lambs and it is a *by-product* of meat production. Vegetarian rennet is obtained from non-animal sources. Cheeses that are made using vegetarian rennet are known as vegetarian cheeses.

Vegetarian rennet

There are three main varieties of vegetarian rennet: microbial, plant, and fermentation-based.

△ **Microbial rennet** is the most common alternative to traditional rennet and is derived from moulds and fungi. It may also be genetically modified.

△ **Plant or vegetable rennet** comes from plants that have coagulating properties, such as fig, nettle, artichoke and thistle. Many Spanish and Portuguese ewe's milk cheeses use thistle as the coagulant and are known to have a unique piquant flavour. The most famous ones are Torta de la Serena, Azeitao, and Serra da Estrella.

⚠ **Fermentation-based rennet** is created by isolating rennet genes from animals and introducing them into certain bacteria, fungi or yeast to make them produce the coagulating enzyme called chymosin. The resulting genetically modified organism (GMO) is killed off after fermentation and then the necessary enzyme is extracted from the remaining broth. The proper name for this type of coagulant is fermentation-produced chymosin (FPC). Even though the process starts using GMOs, the resulting rennet does not contain any GMO or any of its DNA.

Rennet-less cheeses

A small proportion of cheeses are rennet-less. Many soft cheeses are produced without using any rennet and therefore are naturally vegetarian. In this case milk is coagulated with acid, such as citric acid, lactic acid or vinegar. Cream cheese, paneer and cottage cheese are normally made by acidification. However, if you want to avoid traditional rennet, look for a 'vegetarian' notice on the packaging.

Milk

The important first step in making any high-quality product is sourcing the highest quality raw materials. In cheese-making, using quality milk is pivotal, especially if we bear in mind that cheese is essentially seriously dehydrated and concentrated milk. Before we get to the quality aspect of milk, let us look at the possible types of milk that may be used for making cheeses. The most common ones are:

- △ Cow's milk
- △ Goat's milk
- △ Ewe's milk
- △ Buffalo's milk

There are also cheeses that are made from a blend of milks. This tradition was most likely borne out of need during the times of the year when a certain type of milk was in short supply or completely unavailable. For instance, an Italian cheese called La Tur is made from a blend of cow's, sheep's and goat's milk throughout the year but during the winter it contains more cow's and sheep's milk. In the summer, more goat's milk is added to the blend. Another famous mixed milk cheese is Cabrales from Asturias in Spain. Throughout its long history, it has been primarily made from a blend of cow's, sheep's and goat's milk depending on their seasonal availability. Today, however, we can find pure cow's milk Cabrales on the market as well. Both varieties of this strong blue cheese are amazingly powerful, but for me the blended one has the edge.

Proximity of milk

The choice of milk type and its quality cannot be underestimated at the pre-making stage. The proximity of milk supply and the exact origin of milk play a central role in forming the ultimate character of cheese and determine whether it becomes a fine cheese or a commodity destined for supermarket shelves.

Small cheesemaking farms use their own animals' milk (producing a farmhouse cheese), whereas artisanal cheese operations have to source milk from other farms *nearby* (producing an artisan cheese). Large creameries source milk from large farms across the country, producing industrial cheese.

The key difference here is the distance that milk travels to get to a cheesemaking vat, as well as the size of the herd or flock. The shorter the distance and the smaller the herd, the more likely it is that the quality of milk will be high and it will be used to produce a fine cheese. The greater the distance and the larger the herd, the more likely it is that milk will need to be pasteurised or even sterilised, which will inevitably have detrimental effects on the flavour and character of the cheese.

Because their milk travels for significantly shorter distances, if at all, it is much easier for farmhouse and artisan cheesemakers to control the quality of their milk. Farmhouse cheesemakers can pump their milk directly from the milking animal to the cheesemaking vat, so they have an opportunity to use raw milk and save all the natural vitamins and minerals, as well as microflora responsible for the creation of unique and complex flavours in cheese. Large creameries that bring milk from far away must pasteurise their milk to ensure its safety, which negatively affects not only its organoleptic properties (the aspects that are experienced by your senses, including taste, sight, smell and touch) but also its nutritional composition.

On feed quality and pasteurisation

We all have heard the adage, 'We are what we eat', meaning that the quality of our health is determined by the quality of our diet. The same thing is true for dairy animals. It is not only their health that is affected by their feed quality but also their milk, and as a result cheese made from it.

The best feed for dairy animals – cows, sheep and goats – is grass. Grass-fed milk is known to be more flavoursome and nutritionally rich. Cheeses made from grass-fed animals' milk are believed to be the most complex, nuanced and wholesome. In the absence of grass, as is the case in the winter months, animals can be fed hay, but the flavour intensity and even colour of winter cheeses can be more subdued. Silage is believed to negatively affect cheese flavour and even texture. As a result, many European cheesemakers ban its use for legally protected cheeses, such as Comté and Parmigiano Reggiano.

Let's take a look at heat treatment of milk. On the surface, the difference between raw milk cheeses and pasteurised cheeses is the treatment of milk before cheesemaking. Raw milk is not heat-treated, whereas pasteurised milk is heated to over 63°C for at least 30 minutes before cheesemaking.

However, it is more complex than that and the devil is in the microscopic detail. It is in the complexity, invisible to the naked eye, that hides within the milk. Raw milk is a living substance, full of enzymes and microflora. When gathered straight from healthy animals and pumped directly into the cheesemaking vat, this milk will not only produce a cheese that possesses more complexity in its flavour and aroma, it will also be more wholesome and offer extra health benefits such as digestive enzymes, probiotic bacteria and vitamins and minerals. When handled correctly, raw milk has a natural ability to keep bad bacteria in check by outnumbering them with good ones.

Pasteurised milk is believed to have one advantage – it is considered safe. However, even that is not necessarily true. Damaging the natural 'checks and balances' system by killing off *all* bacteria (good and bad) during pasteurisation means that milk becomes susceptible to an invasion of bad microbes. From the safety viewpoint it is more important that the milk is handled correctly by cheesemakers.

Complexity-wise, pasteurised milk will always offer a more subdued experience when compared to the raw milk cheeses. That said, there are numerous examples of scrumptious pasteurised cheeses, such as La Tur, Dunlop and Gorgonzola Dolce. If I had to choose one or the other, however, I would always select raw milk cheeses, as they are far more complex, satisfying and wholesome.

Industrial vs fine cheesemakers

Now we have an understanding of the cheesemaking process and the essential ingredients of cheese, let's look at the differences between fine cheese (also known as farmhouse and artisan) and industrial cheese, the kind of cheese you might find in large slabs in the supermarket. Naturally occurring variability of milk through the year has the potential to significantly complicate the cheesemaking process. The way a producer deals with this variability puts them in one of two groups: industrial cheesemakers versus fine cheesemakers. To put it bluntly:

△ Industrial cheesemakers fight the variability of milk.

△ Fine cheesemakers embrace the variability of milk.

As a result, the two groups start the production process with entirely different ingredients:

△ Industrial cheesemakers start with milk that is pasteurised or even sterilised, void of micro-organisms that contribute to the flavour and aroma development. Therefore, they have to introduce flavour to their products by other means. For example, smoking or enriching with fruit and other flavour additives.

△ Fine cheesemakers start with milk that includes a microcosm of micro-organisms and enzymes that will play a central role in the flavour and aroma development.

Not only are the raw materials strikingly different in composition, the way they get treated during the cheesemaking process is contrasting too:

△ In industrial production of cheese, almost the whole process is automated and carried out by machines.

△ Fine cheesemakers are actively involved in making the cheese. The pivotal steps, like determining the readiness of the curd for cutting, always get undertaken by humans and not machines.

MAHON
Menorcan cheese that can be
produced industrially and artisanally

The resulting cheeses have striking differences:

△ Industrial producers make cheeses that tend to have a mild, bland, natural flavour and aroma. They contain few if any health benefits and do not evolve or improve with age.

△ Fine producers make cheeses that have a naturally occurring complex and lingering flavour and aroma. Health benefits of milk including vitamins and minerals are often retained, and they develop other health benefits during production, such as probiotic bacteria, which evolve and change with maturation.

The aim of the industrial producer is to turn out a product in vast quantities that is always the same, at a price that is affordable to everyone. In doing so, they sacrifice the complexity, variability and character that comes from respect for the milk and the development of processes that work with its characteristics instead of trying to tame them.

On the other hand, if milk's complexity is embraced and encouraged to shine by the skilful approach of a cheese-maker, that is an example of fine cheesemaking. In their book, *Mastering Cheese*, Max McCalman and David Gibbons quote the former American Cheese Society President, Allison Hooper, as saying:

'In artisanal cheesemaking, to maintain quality, you do not alter your raw materials; rather, you adjust your recipe. In industrial cheesemaking, the opposite is true: the raw materials are altered - with various treatments and additives - in order to conform with the recipe.'[7]

Put simply, fine cheese can only be produced by humans. Outsourcing the entire process to automated machinery will always lead to inferior results. It takes an eye for detail and knowledge of chemistry and biology to produce a fine cheese. In addition to the basic milk, starter culture and rennet combination, fine cheese producers rely on imperceptible-to-the-eye ingredients - moulds, yeasts and microflora - and they know how to treat them to create an outstanding product. Milk in its pure raw form

---

7   M McCalman and D Gibbons, *Mastering Cheese: Lessons for Connoisseurship from a Maître Fromager* (Clarkson Potter, 2009)

contains a whole universe of microflora. As complex as it is unpredictable and variable, it must be handled correctly. That is where the talent, experience and craftmanship of the cheesemaker come into play.

Spotlight on cheese: COMTÉ

Comté: the crème de la crème of French cheese

Comté to the French is what cheddar is for the British. It flows in their blood, which is unsurprising as this cheese has been around for over 1,000 years. Today there are over 2,500 dairy farms with the sole focus of producing quality milk for this amazing cheese. They do not spread themselves thin by also making the cheese.

By law, only two breeds of cow can be used for milk that goes into Comté - Montbéliarde and French Simmental (95% and 5% respectively) - and each cow must have at least a hectare (2.47 acres) of grass to feed on in the summer, resulting in raw milk that is wholesome and intense in flavour. Use of silage is not permitted even during the winter months, as it is believed to have adverse effects on the milk and the cows' wellbeing and all types of GMO are also banned.

The milk can only travel a maximum of eight miles to reach the dairy, of which there are about 140. The process is still controlled by humans, rather than machines, with cheesemakers using only their eye and hand to assess the readiness of the curd. Copper vats are a must in any Comté dairy as they are believed to impart superior flavour and composition to the cheese.

COMTÉ
The most beloved French cheese

The minimum legal maturation requirement for Comté is four months, but for such a large wheel of cheese, which weighs on average 40 kg, this is a short period of time. For cheese with a rich and profound flavour that will shine on a cheeseboard, seek out Comté aged for a minimum of twenty months.

At four months old, all wheels of Comté undergo a grading test. Those that score over fourteen points are considered premium and receive a green band around the cheese. Those scoring twelve to fourteen points get a brown band, and those that score under twelve points are excluded from the official labelling. For a cheeseboard, I would only recommend using the extra mature (twenty months or more) green label Comté, whereas the brown label can be used for cooking and melting.

If you compare supermarket-bought Comté with one bought in a speciality cheese shop you will discover that the flavour intensity, texture and aroma will be significantly stronger, more profound and lingering. The primary reasons are a significant age difference and packaging, as vacuum packing negatively affects all organoleptic aspects of cheese.

Some cheese lovers may think of enjoying Comté as 'been there, done that' but I encourage you to keep your eyes and most importantly palates open to trying new Comtés, as they can vary hugely, from producer to producer, from season to season and even from mountain slope to mountain slope. I once had the great pleasure of taking part in a Comté masterclass during the Bra Cheese Festival, which turned out to be one of the most eye-opening gastronomic experiences I've ever had. During the masterclass, we were treated to five Comtés that varied not only in age, but also in the elevation and aspect of the mountain the cows grazed on, and the season during which they were made. The flavour, aroma and texture differences were at first easy to miss for the untrained eye but the more we tasted them and compared them to each other, the more obvious and apparent the differences became. Since then, I have paid close attention to these subtle differences when tasting my fine cheeses and I encourage you to do the same.

How to enjoy Comté

△ Four- to eighteen-month-old cheeses display clean milky and buttery flavours and are best enjoyed on sandwiches, salads and general cooking where a melting cheese is required.

△ Eighteen to twenty-four-month-old wheels develop a more complex flavour with toasty, nutty, meaty notes and are best enjoyed with medium-bodied white and red wines, as well as sparkling wines complemented with fresh fruit, nuts and charcuterie.

△ Twenty-four to forty-month-old wheels pack the most complex flavours and aromas that can include chocolatey, fudgy and even peppery notes. The paste is generously dotted with white protein crystals. Enjoy with your best medium-to-full-bodied red and white wines, but for a special treat serve it with a bottle of Vin Jaune or vintage champagne.

SUMMARY

In this chapter, we have travelled through time to explore the history of cheese. We have also looked at an overview of how cheese is made and the importance of quality ingredients in fine cheese.

We've looked at the differences between raw and pasteurised milk cheeses and industrial vs fine cheesemaking, and the reason why supermarket cheeses taste less complex and profound than their farmhouse and artisan counterparts.

In Chapter 3 we will begin the first step of the Cheese Connoisseur's Way. Here we will learn about how to develop a cultured taste for cheese and begin learning about how to categorise and select your fine cheeses.

Step 1: Cultured Taste

Many of us understand the importance of having legislation that is designed to protect consumers from being misled. We should not, however, expect consumer protection legislation to catch up with reality any time soon. It is up to us, the consumers, to get enlightened about the foods we are eating and to distinguish between what is good and safe for us and what must be avoided at all costs. That is why this first step of the Cheese Connoisseur's Way is so important. In this chapter, you will develop an eye for quality and gain a deeper understanding of how fine cheeses are characterised and described. This is the first important step on your way to lasting cheese happiness.

A lot of people have become aware of the dangers of the powerful multi-billion corporation-sponsored marketing. But large numbers of consumers can still be tricked by clever marketing into thinking that 'farmhouse' cheddar from a supermarket was actually made *on a farm*. It's the same with greenwashing practices, where a company passes products off as 'eco', 'natural' or 'bio' without them being truly ecologically sound.

We are spoiled for choice these days but the downside is that it is easy to get information overload and make bad decisions. It is still the products with the loudest and most expensive marketing that win the battle for customers' attention and not those of superior quality. This causes a problem for cheese. Farmhouse and artisan cheese, that is.

Farmers do not have marketing budgets, as a general rule. Their products can be overshadowed by inferior but highly marketed products. As consumers we need to be hyper-aware and discerning when it comes to quality levels in cheese to ensure we enjoy the right kind of cheese - fine cheese, and not something that may be passed off as such.

Fine cheese terminology

It exasperates me when words like 'artisan' and 'traditional' get thrown around frivolously. Supermarkets and big food brands intentionally use this labelling to evoke the idea of the 'naturalness' of their food, but this is a marketing ploy. It gets even trickier when some smaller producers use the same terminology, even though their end product is as close to mass-produced cheese as one can get. Words like 'artisan', 'fine', 'traditional' and 'vintage' are not protected by law in the UK. Anyone can use them on their products and that misleads people into thinking that some cheeses are better than they actually are. It is important to recognise that simply spotting words like 'artisan' and 'farmhouse' on a product is not enough to ensure its high quality or fine cheese status. There has to be substance behind those claims.

These are my personal definitions of 'farmhouse cheese' and 'artisan cheese' (collectively known as fine cheese):

△ Farmhouse cheese is made in a traditional way where the key stages of the process are performed by a professional cheesemaker and the cheese is the product of one farm. That means that the milk for cheesemaking came from the same farm where the cheese was crafted.

△ Artisan cheese is made in a traditional way where the key stages of the process are performed by a professional cheesemaker, but the milk is sourced from *nearby* farm(s).

Both farmhouse and artisan cheeses are allowed to mature slowly to develop their full flavour and aroma. These definitions are only applicable and usable in a speciality cheese shop setting.

Supermarkets do not use these words in the same way. To ensure you are buying 'farmhouse' or 'artisan' cheeses I encourage you to visit specialist cheese shops. Remember that with clever wording and marketing spin, any product, including cheese, can sound delicious and high quality. It is good to check whether there is substance behind any marketing claims but using specialist retailers will help you save time doing your own research. Supermarkets play a crucial role in our society and are good at providing affordable products, but one should never expect to find the most complex cheeses there.

Is fine cheese only about where the milk comes from, quality raw ingredients and cheesemaking practices? I would argue that the *finest* cheeses have *all* of the following six ingredients:

△ They come from great milk, as we discussed in Chapter 2, and animal welfare and feed are of paramount importance.

△ They are made in a traditional way by masters of the cheesemaking craft.

△ They are properly and slowly matured.

△ They are full of health benefits, when consumed in moderation. We will look at this in more detail in Chapter 6.

△ They have seasonality.

△ They have *terroir* (taste of place).

What about flavour-added cheeses? Can these be considered fine cheeses? It depends. If a cheese was made using complex milk, traditional methods and is naturally complex and lingering in flavour so it can shine on a cheeseboard in its plain form, and the flavouring was added simply to it to enhance or highlight its natural flavour, then I would call it a fine cheese. Examples are Formaggio Ubriaco Rosso, which is a cow's milk cheese washed in red wine, Basajo, which is a ewe's milk blue washed in dessert wine, and Garlic Yarg, a cow's milk cheese wrapped in wild garlic leaves. On the other hand, if a cheese is made from bland milk void of microbiological complexity and the flavour is added to it by way of apricots, cranberries or walnuts, I do not consider this kind of cheese to be 'fine'.

Fine cheese categories

The fine cheese world is full of variety and that is why there are numerous ways to categorise fine cheeses. They can be sorted by:

△ **Milk:** cow, ewe, goat, buffalo, blended

△ **Milk treatment:** raw, pasteurised, thermised

- ⬦ **Rind:** bloomy, washed, natural, cloth-bound, waxed, flavoured (such as wine-soaked or smoked)

- ⬦ **Age:** fresh, young, semi-mature, mature/aged, extra mature/reserve/vintage

- ⬦ **Texture:** soft, crumbly, semi-firm, firm, hard, pasta filata

- ⬦ **Rennet:** traditional/animal, vegetarian (microbial or plant)

WINSLADE
A soft bloomy rind cheese made from
cow's milk in Hampshire, England

However, categorising cheeses by one feature only, such as milk, doesn't really tell us about the character of the cheese. Moreover, any cheese can belong to more than one of the above categories, leading to confusion. For instance, Munster is a cow's milk cheese, but that doesn't tell us anything about its aromatic nature. If you know that it is a washed rind cheese and that its signature trait is a bright orange rind known for intense pungency, then as a customer you're more likely to know whether you're going to enjoy this particular cheese. Unless you are a cheese professional, you shouldn't worry about remembering all of the above categories. Instead, you should focus on the most prominent feature that has the strongest effect on the character of the cheese. Below you will find a functional classification of fine cheese that will be more useful in finding the cheeses you love in the incredible variety any specialist retailer offers, along with some beverage and condiment recommendations for each variety.

My functional classification breaks fine cheeses down into the following categories:

- △ Fresh
- △ Bloomy rind
- △ Washed rind
- △ Semi-firm
- △ Firm
- △ Hard
- △ Blue

Let's take a closer look at each one.

Fresh

These are young un-aged cheeses. Ideally, they go directly from the cheesemaker to your table and should not be kept in your fridge any longer than a week. Predominant attributes: tart, tangy, moist, creamy and smooth or crumbly. They have no rind. Examples are goat's curd, mozzarella and burrata. Complement these with fresh or dried fruit, honey or jam, light white wines such as Pinot Grigio and Sauvignon Blanc, crisp sparkling wines or wheat beer.

Bloomy rind

These are cheeses that are aged for a few weeks and develop a snowy, fluffy 'blooming' rind. They are buttery, creamy and often mushroomy. The part of the cheese beneath the rind, also known as *paste* or *pâte*, is soft and yielding and may become runny and gooey with age. The rind predominantly consists of *geotrichum candidum* and *penicillium candidum* moulds and is edible. Brie de Meaux and Camembert de Normandie are classic examples of bloomy rind cheeses. Complement these cheeses with fresh or dried fruit, fresh baguette, buttermilk crackers or toasty fruit and nut bread. Suitable drinks range from cider to champagne to fruity red wines and off-dry whites.

Washed rind

The term refers to washing the cheese rind with brine during ageing. The brine composition varies from cheese to cheese. It may consist simply of salt and water or may include beer, wine or spirits. These cheeses develop a pungent aroma and a meaty, creamy paste.

The rind is either vibrant orange or pinkish and is edible. The most famous examples of this type are Époisses de Bourgogne and Munster. Complement this type of cheese with dried fruit and nuts or cured meats, pâtés and olives. Drink aromatic white wines such as Gewürztraminer, cider, wheat beer, ale or Trappist beers.

MORBIER
Semi-firm cow's milk cheese with a washed rind

Semi-firm

Aged for normally two to six months, these cheeses often develop a natural rind or have a washed rind (somewhat drier than the washed rinds in the previous category due to longer ageing). The paste can be pliable and bouncy (but not runny) or it can be moist and crumbly. They have earthy, wet straw aromas and a meaty, nutty taste.

Mountain semi-firm cheeses are fabulous melters. Raclette, Fontina, Tomme de Savoie and Gorwydd Caerphilly are all examples of this type of cheese. Complement these cheeses with dried fruit and nuts, freshly baked sourdough bread, cured meats, pâtés and olives. The flavour intensity of these cheeses may vary so make sure to pick drinks with similar intensity. Wheat beer is more suitable for Gorwydd Caerphilly, Pinot Noir for Tomme de Savoie and oaky Chardonnay for Fontina.

Firm

These cheeses are aged from six months up to a year or even eighteen months, depending on their size. They have a dense paste that is still supple when pressed and normally have a natural rind, which is potentially edible, but not incredibly tasty due to strong earthy notes. Flavours range from fruity to nutty. The paste can be crumbly or smooth depending on the cheesemaking recipe. There are many firm cheeses including Comté, Gruyère, Isle of Mull, and Manchego. Complement them with fresh or dried fruit, chutney, fruit puree, membrillo, cured meats, olives, pâtés and sun-dried tomatoes. Drink medium to full-bodied red wines, such as Chianti, Cabernet Sauvignon and Bordeaux or medium-bodied white wines and craft ales.

Hard

Hard cheeses are aged for at least a year if they are small wheels or up to ten years if made in large wheels. They are often the extra mature varieties of firm cheeses. The crucial difference with firm cheeses is that they are rock hard and don't have any give when pressed. They are crunchy, sometimes grainy, but most notably contain a large number of white crystals in the paste. The flavours are intense and can have sweet, nutty, caramelly and butterscotchy notes. Two prominent examples are Vintage Gouda (four years plus) and Parmigiano Reggiano (three years plus). Complement these with dried fruit, fruit cakes or jams. Drinks may range from medium-bodied red and white wines to full-bodied ones, to coffee and even whisky.

Blue

Blue cheeses are impossible to confuse with other varieties as they have distinctive blue or green veins running through their paste. They are often (but not always) salty, peppery and intense. However, there are also mild blue cheeses that are creamy and nutty and not bitey at all. If you believe you do not like blue cheese it is worth starting to explore them from the milder end of the spectrum (Gorgonzola Dolce, for example) and when you're ready you can move your way up the strength scale. Other well-known examples of blue cheese are Roquefort and Stilton. Blue cheeses shine when they are complemented by sweet condiments such as honey, jam or grape nectar, dried fruit and nuts, or even chocolate. As for drinks, opt for Sauternes, Port, Madeira, late harvest Riesling and Gewürztraminer.

Maturation

Cheese maturation (ageing or *affinage* in French) is a complex chemical process, when ferments and micro-organisms on the inside and outside of the cheese slowly change its composition by breaking down complex molecules into simple ones. During this process, cheese develops its characteristic texture, flavour and aroma. This is probably the most mysterious and artistic stage of cheesemaking. More often than not, one gains knowledge in this field through experience or trial and error, and therefore it takes time.

The specialist who matures cheese is known as an *affineur* in French. They must know the techniques required to look after each particular variety of cheese. They also have to understand chemical changes taking place inside cheeses and what effects manipulations of the ageing environment (particularly in terms of temperature and humidity) may have on them.

Soft cheeses with a white bloomy rind take only a few weeks to mature. The affineur has to make sure that the *penicillium candidum* mould is growing evenly on the surface of the cheese and that there is no wetness developing on either side. These cheeses must be regularly flipped over.

Semi-firm or semi-soft cheeses with their bright orange or pinkish rind are also known as 'washed rind' due to the regular washing of the outside with brine. Rind washing promotes growth of the desired *brevibacterium linens* (the same bacterium that is ubiquitously present on human skin) on the outside of the cheese which, in turn, are responsible for the memorable aroma of these cheeses, as well as their pink-orange rind colour. Brine composition varies from producer to producer, from affineur to affineur, but the most basic brine consists of salt and water, whereas more sophisticated ones can contain alcoholic beverages such as wine, beer or cider, and herbs and spices. Some brines are so unique and special that they are believed to be the crucial ingredient to a cheese's character, as is the case with the famous Swiss Appenzeller. Its herbal brine consists of at least twenty-five different Alpine herbs and is a closely guarded trade secret.

Firm and hard cheeses have to spend extended periods of time in maturing conditions, be it a cellar, cave or a temperature- and humidity-controlled room. These cheeses are only marginally less labour-intensive than soft cheeses, as they still require close monitoring and care and, due to their large size, the process can be physically demanding. All long-maturing cheeses will need to be turned regularly to ensure that they are ageing evenly on both sides and do not develop hard or soft patches. Depending on the exact variety, other techniques may be needed including brushing, mould plucking and rind washing.

Cheese maturation techniques are numerous and as varied as the fine cheeses. But there is one simple rule that is universal for ageing every variety. Constant temperature and humidity should be maintained and their exact ranges will depend on the type of cheese.

Seasonality

Seasonal variability of fine cheese is a fascinating but often underappreciated feature. In a world where we have come to expect everything to be standardised and uniform, this little quirk sometimes throws people off. It is worth remembering that traditional cheese is an agricultural product that is directly affected by two factors:

△ Breeding and lactation cycles of the animals

△ Availability and quality of feed

Just like humans, dairy animals produce milk only after giving birth to their offspring, which for them naturally happens in the spring. A normal lactation cycle would last from spring to autumn. However, goats' and ewes' lactation periods are shorter than cows'.

Large-scale industrial producers that rely on a continuous supply of milk have developed ways of dealing with this by freezing milk, but this negatively affects the composition of the milk and the flavour, texture and aroma of the final cheese. Other ways that cheesemakers (including artisans) can counteract this natural phenomenon is by rotating their breeding flocks and using breeds with different naturally occurring breeding cycles. The most humanely obtained and complex milk comes from animals who are allowed to produce milk according to their natural rhythms. Fine cheeses made from natural late spring to early autumn milk will be excellent, and summer milk cheeses will be the crème de la crème.

Animals' feed also plays a pivotal role in the character and organoleptic qualities of any cheese. If dairy animals are grass-fed, expect the flavour and aroma to be of increased intensity, complexity and depth (cow's milk cheeses will also be golden yellow in colour). Moreover, cheeses made from grass-fed animals' milk have extra health benefits. When fresh grass is no longer available and animals are switched to a different diet – ideally hay, but often other less desirable feed types are involved – the quality and complexity of their milk changes entirely. It's easy to identify these cheeses by their pale colour, especially if they are from cow's milk. Expect these cheeses to be less intense and complex than the ones from summer milk, all other factors, such as age, being equal.

The most outstanding and dedicated cheese producers aim to protect the fundamental role of quality milk. For instance, the legally enshrined rules for making L'Etivaz state that it may only be made when cows are grazing on grass on the Alpine slopes, making the production season run from May to October. Alpine slopes boast an incredible array of herbs and flowers that all add to the organoleptic complexity of milk. After these same cows come back to the valley and are switched over to hay, it becomes illegal to make L'Etivaz. In the past, when the same was the case for Comté, enterprising cheesemakers invented a new cheese made purely with hay-fed cow's milk and called it Vacherin Mont d'Or, cleverly creating another seasonal cheese that nowadays cheese aficionados the world over wait impatiently for.

The most traditional and fine cheeses are subject to variability and seasonality. However, it is entirely possible for a traditional cheese to vary during the season, as many other factors play into the complex cheesemaking equation, including rainfall, or absence of it, as well as the cheesemaker's touch. If maturity adds intensity to cheese, then seasonality adds nuance to it.

Cheese with *terroir*

You may have heard of the French word *terroir*, meaning that a product bears 'a taste of place', used in relation to fine wine. It is possible to apply this term to fine cheese too. We have seen how local floral diversity and an animal's diet affect the character of cheese but there are other factors, such as cultural practices, traditions, climate and terrain that all play into the equation. For instance, if milking goats were munching on chestnut leaves and branches during their outdoor exploits in France, the cheese produced from their milk will have a nuance of chestnuts, as in Tomme de la Chataigneraie. If Alpine and Pyrenean animals migrate up the mountains for the summer and back to the valley for the winter, those cheeses will taste different depending on the elevation and slope aspect where they spend most time. In fact, highly developed and trained palates can taste the difference between the flavours of Comté, for instance, produced at 800m versus 1,500m of altitude, as well as those produced from milk sourced from the eastern and western sides of the mountain.

As we now know, all raw milk is complex. It is teeming with an endless profusion of microbes – both good and sometimes bad. When handled properly and hygienically, natural raw milk will produce intensely flavoured and nuanced cheeses, as discussed in the previous chapter, compared to the ones made with pasteurised milk. The microbiological make-up of milk can easily be influenced by the microbiological make-up of its surrounds. Milk sourced from cows in England will be inhabited by different microflora to milk that is sourced in Switzerland. Consequently, cheeses made in Switzerland taste differently to the ones produced in England. There is a simple scientific explanation. When milk is allowed to sour in both countries naturally (ie, without adding starter cultures) it gets invaded by different types of native microflora unique to the environment around. In traditional cheesemaking, the soured milk is used as a starter for making cheese and the resulting cheeses inherit the character of their starter and literally of their environment.

The fact that Swiss cheeses had an obvious mass appeal with their overt fruitiness got cheesemakers in Britain thinking during the twentieth century. Why don't we make our cheddar taste this fruity, instead of it being sharp and earthy (which can be challenging for modern palates)? All they had to do was to cheat on the traditional starter cultures with commercially produced ones that were derived from the Swiss. Thus, the connection with the land was broken and the 'modern' cheddar was born. Of course, fruity cheddars have a mass appeal and it's a good thing because more people are enjoying cheese. However, it's sad that some of our food heritage is in danger of being lost to satisfy those shoppers who favour certain types of flavours.

Milk also varies compositionally depending on whether it is from a cow, sheep or goat, as well as by breed. Generally, ewe's milk is the richest in micronutrients, vitamins and minerals, whereas goat's milk is the lightest. Cow's milk is somewhere in between. However, certain breeds of cow, such as Jersey cows, can offer milk as rich as ewe's milk, which will have a noticeable effect on the flavour of the cheeses made from it. The complexity of natural raw milk is endless and is one of the key reasons for the complexity of fine cheese. If you'd like to learn more, I recommend a fantastic book written by Bronwen and Francis Percival called *Reinventing the Wheel*. Percival's book is a true eye opener on milk and traditional cheese.

Not every cheese aficionado will want to dig this deep for their everyday gastronomic enjoyment. If you are a bit curious, I encourage you to compare the taste of the same cheese (Comté, for example) at different ages, seasons, years and so on to train your palate to distinguish these variations. Cheese master classes and festivals are a good place to do that. I especially recommend the cheese festival in Bra, Italy that I mentioned in the previous chapter. It is the most electric and exciting place for a cheese lover, with endless farmhouse and artisan cheeses and masterclasses on offer across town. It is a must visit for any cheese connoisseur.

Organic cheese

In recent years there has been increasing hype about organic foods and products. More people recognise that the foods we consume play a major role in our overall health and I completely support that movement. However, while it is true that organic foods and farming are hugely beneficial to us on many levels, it doesn't mean that foods that do not carry an organic certification are automatically bad for us. Also, just because a certain cheese is certified as organic doesn't mean that it will be complex or even delicious. Organic milk, in inexperienced hands, especially if it has been pasteurised, can spell a bland cheese. Just beware.

There are plenty of non-organic cheeses that are amazingly natural and offer all the benefits of organic without the stamp, in addition to their complexity of flavour. The organic certification is an expensive and time-consuming bureaucratic process, which makes it prohibitive, particularly for small producers. Then there are cheeses that have 'naturalness' woven into their DNA. Take L'Etivaz, Gruyère d'Alpage or Berner Hobelkäse, for example. These cheeses are only made from raw milk of grass-fed cows grazing on luscious meadows full of fresh grass, herbs and flowers high up in the Alps that never see any type of chemical sprayed on them. Grass-fed animals' milk is as good as organic. But even more importantly, research has shown that cheese made from grass-fed animals' milk is high in polyunsaturated acids (namely, conjugated linoleic acid, or CLA, which is considered an antioxidant, a cancer fighter and a fat-reducing fat).[8]

'White gold'

Exceptionally high production standards of anything made in Switzerland are legendary and Swiss cheeses are no

8   McCalman, M, *Mastering Cheese: Lessons for Connoisseurship from a Maître Fromager* (Clarkson Potter, 2009)

exception. Despite the fact that some food additives and colourings are permitted by law, since 2002 the Swiss cheesemaking industry has voluntarily banned the use of all artificial colourings and preservatives. This ban is enshrined in the industry code signed every three years by the majority of Swiss cheesemakers (with the exception of those making some fresh, melting and processed cheeses – the kind of cheeses that are destined for large retailers).

The cheese industry code specifically bans:[9]

△ Genetically produced rennet

△ Additives to prevent undesirable fermentation: nisin (E234), lysozyme (E1105), sodium nitrate (E251) and potassium nitrate (E252)

△ Artificial colourings

△ Surface treatment additives: natamycin (E235)

This chemical purity of milk, married with strict animal welfare laws, outstanding feed and regular inspections is the key to producing exceptional milk, which is rightly known as 'white gold'. This white gold is turned into complex and, most importantly, natural cheeses that can rival organic cheeses.

---

9   Cheese from Switzerland, 'Swiss cheese – a natural product free from additives', www.cheesesfromswitzerland.com/en/production/cheese-a-natural-product, accessed April 2021

Spotlight on cheese: Parmigiano Reggiano

Parmigiano Reggiano: crafted, not produced

There are thousands of cheeses in the world, but not many come close to the one and only Parmigiano Reggiano, especially when it comes to uncompromising dedication to milk quality, craftsmanship and centuries-old traditions. Although it appears omnipresent, I feel that many people underappreciate its true quality. There are many nuances that are worth being aware of to procure the best Parmigiano Reggiano.

For over 900 years, this cheese has been produced using only three ingredients: milk, rennet and salt. It was first invented in the Middle Ages by Benedictine and Cistercian monks, who were determined to develop a firm cheese suitable for long preservation. Today, Parmigiano is the only legally protected Italian cheese that has a minimum ageing requirement of twelve months, and often it is matured for much longer.

The magic of authentic Parmigiano begins in the fields of Parma, Reggio Emilia, Modena, Mantua and Bologna, the only regions allowed by law to produce the cheese where cows are allowed to graze on natural fields boasting sixty to seventy varieties of grassing herbs including clover, fescue and sainfoin. The fields receive no chemical treatment, which means amazing biodiversity for the land, as well as the cleanest, most wholesome milk for cheesemaking. Use of silage in cows' diets is banned even during the winter months.

The second magical ingredient of Parmigiano Reggiano is craftsmanship. There are 300 dairies making a mind-boggling 3,700,000 wheels a year, but the same care and attention goes into every single wheel. It is important to bear in mind that natural milk changes from day to day, from season to season. Instead of forcing the milk to comply with the schedule, the expertise of cheesemakers is used to adjust the recipe. In fact, all pivotal parts of the process are performed by humans, not machines. Even the highly labour-intensive cutting of the curd is done by hand, using an ancient instrument known as a *spino*, which looks like a spherical metal mesh attached to a wooden stick. Cheesemakers have to rely on their knowledge and expertise to cut the curd to the same sized granules every time to produce cheeses of consistent texture and quality. Copper vats are also a must in any Parmigiano dairy as they are believed (and this is supported by research[10]) to impart superior flavour and composition to the cheese.

Due to its incredible popularity, Parmigiano Reggiano is one of the most counterfeited and imitated cheeses around world. However, since 1996 it has been protected by European law. Right after the cheese is made, the words 'Parmigiano Reggiano' are inscribed into their wheel rinds. To keep the name, every single wheel of Parmigiano has to undergo an inspection every year. A grader from the

---

10   McDonough, M, 'Why Copper Vats Matter', Culture Blog
        (19 July 2017), https://culturecheesemag.com/cheese-iq/copper-vats-
        cheesemaking, accessed April 2021

Parmigiano Reggiano Consortium inspects each wheel by knocking on it with a small mallet, looking for structural defects that can be identified by an uneven sound. After the grading, one of three stamps will be applied to the rind. The round stamp gets applied to first-grade wheels, the square one to the second-class Parmigiano (*mezzano*), and the triangular stamp disqualifies the cheese from being labelled as 'Parmigiano Reggiano'. The first- and second-class wheels also receive the famous oval fire-branding of the Consortium. From then on, careful and long maturation plays a major part in flavour and aroma development of the cheese.

You may be sold on the greatness of Parmigiano Reggiano but you may also think it's great that it is now available in supermarkets. I'd like to challenge your thinking and encourage you to compare supermarket-bought Parmigiano Reggiano with one bought in a speciality cheese shop. The flavour intensity, texture and aroma of the speciality product will be significantly stronger, more profound and lingering. The primary reasons are the significant age difference and packaging because, as you'll learn in Chapter 4, vacuum packing negatively affects all organoleptic properties of cheese.

How to enjoy Parmigiano Reggiano

△ Twelve-month wheels have a lactic, yoghurt note, as well as floral and herbal notes. Enjoy this cheese with light sparkling wines.

△ Twenty-two to twenty-eight-month cheeses show fresh fruit and citrus notes, as well as some nutty notes. Enjoy with medium-bodied red or white wines.

△ Thirty to thirty-six-month cheeses have a firm crumbly texture with more pronounced notes of spice, such as nutmeg and deeper fruit and nut notes. Enjoy with medium-bodied wines or vintage champagne and complement with honey and fruit.

△ Forty-eight-month (and upwards) Parmigiano has a profound and rich flavour with a hint of pepper and leather in addition to long notes of fruit and nuts. Enjoy with an intense red or white wine, or dessert wines such as Vin Santo.

△ Red Cow Parmigiano Reggiano: the crème de la crème Parmigiano is made with milk of the Red Cow, a dairy breed praised for its outstanding rich, wholesome and aromatic milk. All Parmigiano used to be made only with Red Cow milk, but today it represents only a small fraction of the overall production. There is an additional marking on the wheels of Red Cow Parmigiano reading 'Vache Rosse', which will help you identify it, but a knowledgeable cheesemonger will do the same job. Enjoy Red Cow Parmigiano that has been matured for over thirty months with your best vintage champagne.

SUMMARY

We've looked at the basic information you need to choose quality cheese, in particular the different categories your favourite cheeses fall into. You have also discovered how maturation, seasonality and even topography play their part in the production of fine cheese. Now you will have a sharper eye for detail when selecting your next cheese treat.

Let's move on to Chapter 4 which deals with Step 2 of the Cheese Connoisseur's Way, which is how to get an outstanding service (or curated service) when choosing your favourite cheese.

CHAPTER 4

Step 2: Curated Service

If you really want to raise your cheese game so that you get the best cheeses for your own palate and to share with your family and friends, this second step on curated service is important. We'll cover how to source and buy the best farmhouse and artisan cheese and the mistakes to avoid. Curation is the key to getting the perfect cheese selection *for you* every time. By curation I mean getting personalised and tailored suggestions based on your needs and desires. This kind of service may not be available in every cheese shop, so first we need to understand how to identify retailers that offer this service.

Cheese retailers – specialist vs generalists

On the surface, buying cheese is easy. Google your nearest cheese stockist, go in and buy. Right? Wrong. This simplistic approach can lead to disappointment. Thinking that all cheese retailers are made equal will be to your disadvantage. Shops like garden centres that sell a bit of everything, including cheese, are generalists. Just as there are different kinds of cheese, there are different kinds of cheese shops. Generalists cater to those who demand novelty cheeses enhanced with apricots and cranberries, whereas others cater to those who value complex and lingering cheeses made by artisans from the most complex and nutritionally rich milk available. By the fact that you are reading this book, I'm guessing you are the latter kind of cheese lover. What you need is a specialist cheesemonger, the kind who sells purely farmhouse and artisan cheeses. No cranberry Stilton in sight.

However, even specialist cheese shops have different approaches to the cheese they stock. Some dabble in the muddy waters of cheeses that pretend to be artisan, when in fact they are mass-produced and their flavour is not naturally occurring.

Fine cheese is a 'live' substance and therefore requires high standards of care throughout its life, from milk to selling. Some retailers do not adhere to these standards and store cheeses incorrectly, at the wrong temperatures or unwrapped, or sell them vacuum-packed. I urge you to raise your standards when buying cheese. Farmhouse and artisan cheeses should be cut from the wheel and should not be chopped up into little bits and vacuum-packed. The process of vacuum packing, as great an invention it has been for food safety, is not the fine cheese lover's friend, especially if you are sourcing cheeses for a cheeseboard. Vacuum packing negatively affects the texture, flavour and aroma of cheese. It literally suffocates soft and blue cheeses, making them unrecognisable and almost completely unenjoyable. Firm and hard cheeses do not suffer as much but there is a perceptible difference, especially for those with more refined palates.

As an experiment I encourage you to see it for yourself by going to a supermarket and buying a piece of Roquefort and then get a slice from a specialist cheese shop. I particularly recommend the Roquefort produced by Le Vieux Berger. Not only is the supermarket Roquefort made on a much bigger scale, which generally means less nuance in flavour, it is also vacuum-packed. As a result, it has nothing on Le Vieux Berger, which is made by hand on a family-run farm and is never vacuum-packed. The difference in texture and flavour is eye-opening. The supermarket Roquefort is still a good cheese but it's best used in cooking, whereas Le Vieux Berger Roquefort is a luxury that is destined for a memorable cheeseboard. If you would rather do this experiment with a non-blue cheese, do the same with Ossau Iraty or Comté. I hope the result of this experiment will convince that if you are looking for cheeseboard cheeses you should source them from specialist retailers.

Specialist cheese paper

Fine cheese is a precious thing. It needs great care, not only during the cheesemaking and maturing process, but also in the hands of retailers and then final consumers. A good cheese retailer not only takes care of their stock while it's at the shop, but they also care about their cheeses' destiny *after* they are sold. In other words, they pay close attention to what they wrap their cheeses in for retail.

PE coated paper (also known as duplex) is the best type of paper to store cheeses in at home. Duplex paper lets cheeses breathe without suffocating them, but it also doesn't let them dry out too quickly. I have done extensive comparative testing of it with other types of wrapping materials including cling film, wax paper and foil. In my tests, out of these three materials, foil performed in a similar way to the duplex paper and cheeses stayed in excellent shape for at least two weeks, whereas in wax paper and in cling film cheeses dried out too quickly. As a result they not only lost their texture, but also flavour and aroma.

Duplex specialist paper has a small drawback. It is made of a layer of paper and an ultra-thin layer of polyethylene, so it is not recyclable. I am sure that anti-plastic campaigners are gasping in horror at this notion, but please bear with me.

Firstly, *any* type of food wrapping, even those that are fully recyclable to begin with, if smeared with food residue (which is 100% the case with soft cheeses) cannot be recycled. Secondly, fine cheese costs a premium – why would you want any of it go to waste, which would be the case if you stored it in something as porous as wax paper? One wouldn't dream of ageing or storing a bottle of fine wine such as Petrus in a plastic bottle, so why treat fine cheese with any less consideration? In my expert opinion, duplex paper is the best for cheese storage as it significantly extends its life in your fridge and therefore your continued enjoyment.

If you are still not convinced that duplex paper is the way to go, then an alternative is to bring a reusable box with you when you go shopping for cheese. As a cheesemonger, I'm more than happy to place your wedges in a box – just be sure to consume your cheeses within a short period of time, as they will dry out quicker than if they were wrapped in cheese paper.

Curated cheesemonger service

Now that you are going to be extra discerning about the cheese shops you frequent, it's time to discuss what exactly to do when you are there. I see it every day – people come to us and are completely overwhelmed by choice. They often feel embarrassed to admit that they don't know cheese very well and they need help. If not stopped, they end up panic buying cheeses they don't even know they will like. This is not the way to find the perfect cheeses for your taste, favourite drink or occasion.

The alternative is to use the professional help of a cheesemonger and the key is to *be open* to receiving help. Remember, cheesemongers are not merely human cheese cutting machines, they are cheese professionals. If the cheesemonger is worth their salt, they will ask a few insightful questions that will help them understand your palate and your occasion better and tailor their offering based on your answers. Professional and passionate cheesemongers possess deep knowledge and understanding of their product. They know what raw ingredients were used, what cheeses are in season and what's great on that particular day. Use their expertise to your advantage and you will end up with a far superior experience and, most importantly, outstanding cheese.

One pitfall to avoid is asking your cheesemonger something as generic as, 'What do you recommend?' This question is too broad and as a result you can get, 'We recommend all our cheeses,' in response. But it can also be dangerous because if you're visiting a shop with low stock turnover you may end up with cheeses they are trying to get rid of. So, beware. When I hear that question, I normally say that all the cheeses we stock are my babies and I recommend them all! And that is true. But it does not help you to find *your* perfect cheese. A better way for you to approach this is to say something along these lines:

'I'm planning a dinner party and I would like to blow my foodie guests away with my cheeseboard. I'll be serving red Bordeaux throughout the evening. I would like five off-the-beaten-track cheeses that are varied in texture and flavour and would really impress my guests. I like most cheeses, including blues, but not goat's milk cheeses. What do you recommend?'

Or:

'I'm having my friends over for lunch and because it's my birthday we'll be drinking champagne. I'd like two creamy cheeses, one firm and no blue. What do you recommend?'

Or:

'I would like to buy a treat for myself. I love goat's and sheep's milk cheese and I would like to get two or three different varieties, including blue. What do you recommend?'

That is something I can work with! Providing a lot of information and being completely open about what you like and don't like will help your cheesemonger tailor the offering to suit you perfectly.

If you do not know the exact beverage you are going to have your cheeses with, it's not a problem. Select the cheeses you like and then ask your cheesemonger what they recommend to complement these cheeses. Some extra passionate mongers know about wine, beer and spirits, so to take your cheeseboard experience one step further chat to them about the drinks you may have. If you are teetotal that's not a problem either, as many cheeses can be served with other beverages like tea and coffee.

How often should you buy cheese?

It is best to buy little and often, but it all depends on your proximity to a good cheese shop. If you are lucky to live near a good cheese specialist, like most French people, then shopping for cheese could be a weekly habit that will guarantee the top-notch quality of your fromage. Don't despair if you don't have a chance to pop into a cheese shop regularly, as most farmhouse and artisan cheeses will last, when stored properly in the fridge. We'll discuss proper cheese storage a bit later in this chapter.

Affordable luxury

Fine cheese has a reputation for being on the pricey side, but I hope to convince you that you wouldn't really want it any other way. Rock-bottom prices are only possible at the expense of quality when conveyor-belt production and corner-cutting happen. As we discussed in Chapter 3, fine cheese requires human involvement, as well as care and attention all along its production cycle – from milk to curd to fully matured wheels. It takes dedicated farmers, passionate and skilful cheesemakers, and knowledgeable affineurs with specialist skills and a magic touch to make a cheese really shine on your plate and your palate. If you take the human involvement away, you will end up with a generic cheese, devoid of character, aroma or flavour.

LA PERAL
An artisan blue from Asturias, Spain

Traditional cheesemakers are humble, down to earth and hardworking people, who get up to milk their animals and start making cheese before dawn, work tirelessly through-out the day, and turn wheels by hand, brushing, washing or plucking them if needed. They rarely, if ever, take holidays. I am sure you agree that they deserve a fair remuneration for their efforts. Having worked with cheesemakers and affineurs, I can still remember the sore back I had after hovering over the cheese vat, piling curd into moulds, and the unsocial hour I got up at to brush the cheeses in the maturing cellars in France. The meticulous care, preci-sion, skill and expertise that go into making a traditional cheese can only be compared to making high-quality designer goods. Think of a Chanel bag - its ingredients are of outstanding quality and the craftsmanship is superb. Fine cheeses are the same. When you compare them to luxury goods, only then can you appreciate they are luxury goods themselves, at a fraction of the price. Fine cheese is more expensive than mass-produced cheese but that is (almost literally) comparing chalk and cheese. Products of outstanding quality should be *reassuringly expensive* and they are worth every penny.

Storing your cheese at home

We now know that farmhouse and artisan cheese is a 'live' product, which means that it evolves over time and requires particular cellar-like conditions for its proper maturation. As soon as a cheese leaves those ripening conditions and/or loses its physical wholeness (in other words, it gets cut), it no longer matures and needs to be refrigerated to preserve its freshness and to avoid spoilage. This process is called storage.

Depending on the variety, the conditions and length of storage vary. However, there are general storage rules applicable to all cheese types. The guidelines below will help you to store cheeses properly at home to extend their longevity and ensure they are safe to eat:

△ Keep fine cheese in a dedicated vegetable drawer in your fridge where it will be away from draughts and enjoy its own micro-climate.

△ Keep your cheeses wrapped in specialist cheese paper such as duplex paper. It allows cheese to breathe and not dry out or suffocate at the same time. Foil may be used as an alternative, but avoid using wax paper and plastic wrap, especially if you want to keep cheeses fresh for longer. Under-wrapping cheese in cling film will dry them out, whereas over-wrapping will suffocate them.

△ Each variety should be wrapped separately to avoid cross-contamination of flavour.

△ Do not keep other foods in the same compartment with fine cheese, especially if those foods are highly aromatic. Cheese can absorb other aromas and therefore lose its own original character.

△ Do not freeze fine cheese. It negatively affects the texture and flavour nuances of cheese.

How long is it safe to keep cheese at home? It depends on the variety and ripeness/maturity of the cheese when you buy it. You can ask your cheesemonger when purchasing but here are the general guidelines:

△ Soft and semi-firm: up to two weeks.

△ Blue: up to two weeks.

△ Firm and hard: up to thirty days.

△ Fresh rind-less cheeses are not for keeping. Follow the date on the packaging or consume within five days after production.

Rinds: Can I eat that?

At every single one of my tasting events, I get asked about rinds, more specifically whether you can eat them or not. There are so many different varieties that it's hard to give one definitive answer that will apply to them all, but I will try to give you a few pointers:

△ Do not eat the rinds that have cloth, wax or plastic on them. It's pretty obvious, but it needs to be said.

△ On soft cheeses, the rinds are really considered to be 'skins'. As a result, they are an integral part of the cheese and its character. Bloomy, washed rinds and skins on soft goat's milk cheeses are definitely edible and are delicious.

△ On firm cheeses, the rinds are generally 'natural', meaning they are just dried out cheese. These rinds can also be called crusts and their job is to save the cheese inside from drying out during its long maturation. Natural rinds are potentially edible, but you may find them to be quite hard and earthy. Here the choice is yours - try the rind and if you like it, you are welcome to eat it. It is not going to do you any harm.

△ Blue cheeses can have natural rinds or they can be rind-less. For the ones with natural rinds, refer to the previous point. The rind-less blues are usually covered in foil, which makes them get a little bit wet and smelly on the outside of the cheese. Personally, I tend to cut these bits off, but again the choice is yours – you can try it and see what you think.

Spotlight on cheese: ROQUEFORT

Roquefort: the not so hidden gem

When I help my customers select cheeses for their cheeseboard and we get to the decision about the big note at the end, also known as a blue cheese, more people than not quickly turn down any suggestion of Roquefort by saying, 'Oh, I've tried that.' To which I as quickly say, 'But have you tried Roquefort Le Vieux Berger yet?' With Roquefort the devil is in the detail, as tends to be the case with many other well-known cheeses. The philosophy of a particular producer will dictate nuances of flavour and texture.

Roquefort was first made in the south of France and there is a lovely legend around its origin. It is believed that a young shepherd got distracted by a beautiful girl and left his lunch provisions of bread and fresh cheese in a cave. When he returned, the bread and cheese had gone mouldy but the cheese tasted even better. Thus, Roquefort was born. This story may be fictitious, but it is a fact that *penicillium roqueforti* mould is naturally present in caves. To this day, some producers use locally baked rye bread to cultivate *penicillium roqueforti*, which then gets ground and added to milk to inoculate it with this delicious mould.

Roquefort was the first cheese in France to receive legal protection in 1925. By law, today it must be made only from the raw milk of Lacaune ewes, who are known for their rich milk, and every wheel must be matured in the caves of Roquefort-sur-Soulzon. One cannot underestimate the pivotal role of these caves. They are a perfect environment for blue cheese maturation. All year round they are at a constant temperature of 10–12°C and have a high humidity of 95%. The most unique feature, however, is the *fleurines*, the fissures in the rock that serve as natural air vents, providing gentle circulation of air essential for cheese maturation.

Currently there are seven producers of Roquefort. They vary in size and therefore their resulting cheeses vary in nuance and complexity. Each producer gets to choose from 700 varieties of *penicillium roqueforti* strains, which ultimately adds to the unique alchemy of their recipe. The largest volume producer is the Société des Caves de Roquefort, a subsidiary of Lactalis, a massive international conglomerate with operations in fifty-five countries. It holds the largest number of caves and accounts for 60% of all Roquefort production. Roquefort Papillon is the second largest producer by the number of caves and offers for different market levels. The other five producers are Carles, Gabriel Coulet, Fromagerie Aquitaine, Vernières Frères, and Le Vieux Berger. Each hold one cave and have a substantially smaller share of the market but they are held in high regard when it comes to attention to detail and outstanding quality.

It is worth trying the cheeses from all seven producers to explore the subtle - and sometimes not so subtle - differences between them. My favourite, by far, is Le Vieux Berger and that's the one I carry at my shop. Le Vieux Berger is the smallest producer and is still a family enterprise run by fewer than ten workers. Since 1923, the Combes family has been uncompromising on the founding principles of manual craftsmanship and tradition. You will not find their Roquefort in supermarkets, which means it is always cut from the wheel, never vacuum-packed and therefore retains its gorgeous rich texture and intense flavour.

How to enjoy Roquefort

There are many ways to use Roquefort in cooking, both in sweet in savoury dishes, as it can go in dips, mousses, soups, pies and even cakes. The more exquisite your wedge of Roquefort is, the more reason to savour it slowly as part of a cheeseboard and pair it with your best dessert wine such as Sauternes, Monbazillac or late harvest Gewürztraminer.

SUMMARY

In this chapter, we have learned about Step 2 of the Cheese Connoisseur's Way to cheese happiness, which is about how to get that personalised service when choosing your fine cheese. Essential to this is to find the right cheese shop, where your cheesemonger will help and advise you on the type of cheese to make your cheeseboard a success at any event. We've looked at the essential questions to ask to get the right advice and, following that, how you can store your cheese so that it remains fresh for as long as possible.

Now you know how to choose fine cheeses, we will move on to Part Two, which is about how to savour your cheese. This brings us to the third element in our model: continuous enjoyment.

PART TWO
SAVOUR

Part Two includes the final three steps of the Cheese Connoisseur's Way and will be dedicated to learning about how to get the most out of your fine cheese experiences and how to savour cheese. You will get more pleasure from every bite, *savour* cheese without guilt and use every cheese experience to enrich your life. You'll pick up some useful tips on how to pair and match your cheese with wine and some fail-proof cheeseboard ideas to implement at your next dinner party.

CHAPTER 5

Step 3: Continuous Enjoyment

As humans, we are wired to seek comfort. Any extremes in our circumstances – extreme abundance or extreme deprivation – can be the cause of severe stress for our minds and bodies, especially if sustained over long periods of time or repeated regularly. Going from extreme starvation to overabundance of food is not sustainable or good for us. A much better way for both our bodies and our minds is having an easily sustainable rhythm of being and eating. In this chapter, we will look at Step 3 of the Cheese Connoisseur's Way, which is how we can have continuous enjoyment of cheese throughout the year by maintaining balance. Here you will explore how a manageable, sustainable and continuous rhythm to your cheese consumption is much better for you than overindulging in cheese once a year at Christmas and then depriving yourself of it for the rest of the year, unlike the Swiss, French and Italians, who consume cheese year-round and have enviably long lives.[11]

Cheese in a balanced diet

Before we can even talk about having cheese as part of a healthy balanced diet, we need to understand what a balanced diet is. The concept of balanced diet changes depending on who you ask. The phrase is so overused that

---

11   Life expectancy in Switzerland is 83.79 years, in Italy 83.1, in France 82.7.
     Source: https://datacommons.org/ranking/LifeExpectancy_Person/Country

it has lost its meaning and, as a result, the whole concept is rarely practised. The good news is that we can create our own definition of a balanced diet with fine cheese as part of it. Our definition of a balanced diet will ensure we are eating well for our physical selves but also for our psychological selves, as we need to be sure that we are not only feeding our tummies but also our souls.

As a foundation to our definition, I'd like to use the *Eatwell Guide, published by the British Nutrition Foundation in 2016.*[12]

The main dietary messages are as follows:

- △ Eat at least five portions of a variety of fruit and vegetables every day.

- △ Base meals on higher fibre starchy foods like potatoes, bread, rice and pasta.

- △ Have some dairy or dairy alternatives such as soya drinks.

- △ Eat some beans, pulses, fish, eggs, meat and other protein.

- △ Choose unsaturated oils and spreads, and eat them in small amounts.

- △ Drink at least six to eight glasses of fluid a day.

While the *Eatwell Guide* provides a good starting point, it misses out two important ideas that would help strengthen

---

12   Eatwell Guide: www.nutrition.org.uk/healthyliving/healthydiet/eatwell.html

our mental health and make it more applicable for lifelong use. The missing ingredients are:

△ Quality of produce

△ Importance of little treats

As we discussed in Chapter 3, the quality of cheese can vary greatly, which will affect nutrients and health outcomes. The same principle applies to all the food you choose to eat. You may be opting for lettuce and lean meats from large fast-food chains but they will not be nearly as beneficial to your body as the farmhouse equivalents. The former are likely to be full of additives, flavour enhancements, hormones and chemicals that are necessary to produce food on a mass scale, while the latter will provide pure unadulterated nutrients for your cells. Keep your eye out for quality, whatever you choose to eat.

I'm also a strong believer in including 'little treats for the soul' in my diet. The two key elements are portion control and frequency. The more frequently you have your little indulgences, the less likely you will be to overindulge. For instance, if I were to have chocolate once in a blue moon, I would probably eat the entire bar. As I can have it whenever I want, I'm completely happy with two or four squares. The same idea applies to fine cheese. Because I can have it whenever I want, I usually choose to have my treat at the weekend and stop eating it before I'm too full.

I am not a physician, nutritionist or psychologist, but having had my share of struggles with food and health, and having found a sustainable diet solution, I like to share to help others. What makes my approach to food and weight sustainable is a balanced inclusion of *foods for health* and *foods for the soul*.

Hence, I'd like to introduce you to my 80/20 principle. In my head I divide all the food I consume into two broad categories:

1. For health - this constitutes over 80% of everything I eat.

2. For pleasure - this constitutes no more than 20%.

This rule may be applied to every meal, every day and every week. In every meal, I aim to have 80% of health-giving foods such as greens, vegetables, fibre and lean protein but I also allow myself little indulgences - some sauce, chips or dessert. Of course, some days the rule will be broken. That's OK, because it can be balanced out over the course of the week. The point is to aim for that balance without being too militant about it, as it is a sure way to kill the joy of eating.

Nutritional composition of cheese

The French consider cheese, bread and wine the 'Holy Trinity' of the table. Together these three foods become a balanced combination of nutrients for a complete wholesome meal, containing protein, fats and carbohydrates.

Cheese, as we know, is essentially a highly concentrated form of milk. As a result, it inherits from milk a large spectrum of healthful nutrients and micronutrients. The dominant nutrients of cheese are proteins, fats and water. It also contains good amounts of some crucial vitamins and minerals.

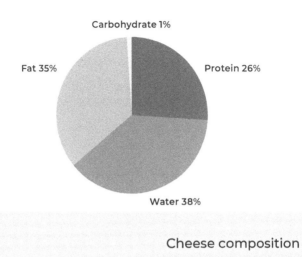

Cheese composition

Protein

Milk's main protein is *casein*. The word protein has Greek origins – it comes from the word 'prota', meaning 'of primary importance'. Proteins are some of the most essential nutrients that our bodies need to stay healthy. They provide the building blocks of body tissue and also serve as a source of energy. Protein is critically important for normal growth of children and for recovering from malnutrition and post-operation situations. During human digestion, proteins break down into amino acids. Our bodies can produce some amino acids but cannot produce others. These are called essential amino acids and we must get them from food. The great news is that cheese is full of essential amino acids, as the protein breakdown process happens during cheese maturation. The most notable amino acid is *tyrosine*, which is linked to giving us a positive mental boost from eating cheese. So if you think that eating cheese makes you happy, you are correct and we can thank tyrosine for that. Some studies have also shown that tyrosine is helpful during periods of sleep deprivation, stress, cold, prolonged work or fatigue and appears to improve physical and cognitive performance.[13]

Lactose

Milk sugar, also known as lactose, is nearly completely removed from the cheese curd during the cheesemaking process. During the early stages of the process, lactose gets converted into lactic acid and the remaining lactose is drained out with whey. The traces of lactose left trapped in the cheese curd break down as the cheese matures. The more mature the cheese is, the less lactose it has.

Lactose is present in milk from cows, sheep, goats and buffalo, so the common misconception that goat's milk is better for lactose-intolerant people is not necessarily true. The best way to avoid lactose is to go for firm or hard mature cheeses, no matter what milk they are. Soft cheeses, which are generally not matured for long and do not have as much whey or lactose removed from them may still contain traces of lactose. Depending on the consumer's sensitivity to lactose, they can still be enjoyed. But if the person is extremely intolerant to milk sugar, it is best to go for the hardest and most mature cheeses. Examples of the 'safe' cheeses are extra mature Gruyère, Comté, Beaufort, Parmigiano Reggiano (two years upwards) and Vintage Gouda.

---

13   M McCalman and D Gibbons, *Mastering Cheese: Lessons for Connoisseurship from a Maître Fromager (Clarkson Potter, 2009)*

Fats

Fat is associated with being harmful. As a result, many people try to completely eradicate it from their diets and feel guilty when eating delicious foods like cheese. This approach is flawed and can have negative health effects. As humans, we need fats as:

△ A source of energy

△ A source of essential fatty acids our bodies cannot make

△ A way to absorb fat-soluble vitamins A, D, E and K

△ A way to protect internal organs from external shocks

△ A way to maintain body temperature and help normal cell function

The main types of fat found in food are saturated and unsaturated fats (mono- and polyunsaturated). The official NHS guidance recommends cutting down on foods and drinks that are high in saturated fats, as eating *too much* saturated fat can raise 'bad' cholesterol.

Cheese is on the list of foods that are high in saturates, which also includes other delicious things like sausages, butter, ice cream and cake. On the bright side, saturated fats can contribute up to 11% of our food energy so cheese doesn't need to be completely eradicated from our diet and can be enjoyed year-round.[14] All we need to do is pick our saturated indulgences wisely, enjoy them in moderation and balance them out with recommended health foods.

In addition to saturated fat (which makes up two-thirds of its fat content), cheese also contains monounsaturated, polyunsaturated fat and some trans fats. Polyunsaturated fat in cheese is credited with lowering heart-attack risk.[15] Cheeses made with grass-fed cow's milk are especially high in conjugated linoleic acid (a type of polyunsaturated fat) which is considered an antioxidant; a cancer fighter and a fat-reducing fat.[16]

It seems unfair that today cheese is often implicated in serious health issues such as obesity and heart disease. Cheese has been around for thousands of years, whereas the prevalence of obesity and heart disease has increased only in the last century. The most likely culprit is not traditional cheese but processed and mass-produced foods that are the products of the new industrial economy. Mass-produced cheese is one of those products. It is noticeably lighter in flavour intensity and complexity, while higher in salt. When trying to get the same satisfaction from mass-produced cheese, people end up over-consuming it in quantity, thus over-consuming salt and fats, which can inevitably lead to weight gain and health issues.

14   British Nutrition Foundation, 'Fat', www.nutrition.org.uk/nutritionscience/ nutrients-food-and-ingredients/fat.html

15   Tunick, M, The Science of Cheese (Oxford University Press, 2014)

16   McCalman, M, Mastering Cheese: Lessons for Connoisseurship from a Maître Fromager (Clarkson Potter, 2009)

When it comes to fine cheese, its exact fat content varies depending on the type of milk used. As a rule of thumb, goat's milk cheeses have the least fat, cow's milk cheeses are in the middle, and sheep's milk cheeses are the richest.

You can check the packaging for the exact fat content in each variety of cheese, but those numbers are often misunderstood by consumers. As a general rule, you need to divide the fat content number by two to get a more accurate idea of how much fat is contained in the cheese. It is a common practice to measure fat in cheese in 'dry matter'. This is the measure taken *after all of the moisture has been completely removed* from cheese.

Take Camembert de Normandie, for example. On its box it normally reads 45% MGP (*matière grasse*) per 100 grams, but it does not mean that 45% of a 100 gram piece is fat. Being a soft cheese, Camembert has a lot of water; before you could measure fat you would have to completely dry the piece out, which would make it lighter in weight at the same time. Essentially, you will end up measuring the fat content in a much smaller than 100 gram piece of cheese. What a lot of cheese lovers fail to recognise is that *what makes soft cheeses soft is moisture* (water), not fat. The fat content in firm and hard cheeses, on the other hand, is higher than in soft because there is less moisture to remove before measuring. However, there are a number of firm/ hard cheeses made from partially skimmed milk, making them naturally 'skinny'. The most famous 'skinny' cheeses are Parmigiano Reggiano and Tomme de Savoie.

Vitamins and minerals

The main minerals in milk, and therefore cheese, are calcium, magnesium and phosphorus. The levels of calcium in cheese are so significant that simply eating cheese on a regular basis would provide enough calcium for a healthy body. Together with phosphorus, calcium plays a central role in building and maintaining healthy bones and teeth. That is why it is important to include cheese in children's and elderly people's diets. Traditional cheese also contains important fat-soluble vitamins – A and D, as well as a complex of B and E vitamins.

Microbes

The ultimate unique selling point (USP) of artisan and farm-house cheeses is that they are 'alive' and everchanging. Raw milk intended for cheesemaking is a living substance and hosts a universe of naturally occurring bacteria and enzymes. It takes the utmost care, knowledge and skill to harvest the right kind of microbes during the cheesemaking process as these will eventually be responsible for the composition of cheese, as well as its texture, flavour and aroma.

In addition to being naturally flavoursome and complex, soft cheeses made with raw milk are also believed to have an extra benefit of being good for the gut as the surviving lactic acid bacteria are considered probiotic.[17] These friendly bacteria feed your gut microbiome. Having a healthy gut microbiome is linked with having a clear mind and higher energy levels.

17　Tunick, M, *The Science of Cheese* (Oxford University Press, 2014)

There are many other friendly bacteria that make farmhouse and artisan cheeses especially flavoursome, moreish and memorable. I would like to mention the most notable ones:

⚠ *Geotrichum candidum*: commonly known as 'dairy mould', it is present in most soft and semi-firm cheeses and plays a big role in flavour and texture development. You can find this mould on cheeses like St. Félicien and La Tur.

⚠ *Penicillium camemberti* and its variant *Penicillium candidum*: the white moulds that grow on soft and semi-firm cheeses and are responsible for texture and flavour development, normally breaking the texture of the cheese from the outside in and changing it from crumbly to smooth and glossy. You can find these moulds on Brie de Meaux, Tomme de Savoie and similar cheeses.

⚠ *Brevibacterium linens*: the hallmark of washed-rind cheeses. These friendly bacteria are responsible for the unique character of washed-rind cheeses, including their flavour, texture and aroma. *B.linens* make the surface of washed-rind cheeses an orange/pinkish colour and help them to develop a memorable farmyardy aroma. The most famous examples are Époisses de Bourgogne and Stinking Bishop.

⚠ *Penicillium roqueforti*: the mould that makes blue cheeses like Roquefort and Stilton blue (however, its variants can also have a green tinge too). *Penicillium roqueforti* breaks down the texture of the cheese, making it softer and creamier on the palate. It also breaks down the fat molecules in cheese to free fatty acids, which are responsible for the development of the piquant flavour and aroma that are so adored by the blue cheese lovers.[18]

I find the world of friendly cheese bacteria absolutely fascinating. It is something that without doubt sets fine cheeses apart from their industrially-produced counterparts.

Health virtues of fine cheese

Let's sum up the health benefits of good cheese:

1. **Packed with essential nutrients and micronutrients:** fine cheese is rich in nutrients like protein, calcium, phosphorus, magnesium, and vitamins A, B2 and B12. These play a crucial role in maintaining a healthy body, such as fortifying bones, teeth, skin and eyes.

2. **It is pure:** there are no chemical preservatives, hard-to-pronounce ingredients or nasty E numbers. There is just nutritious wholesome milk, naturally occurring enzymes and small amounts of salt. Nothing unnatural.

3. **It makes you happy:** we know the taste of it is pure joy, but cheese has been proven to make us

---

18   Kindstedt, P, *American Farmstead Cheese* (Chelsea Green Publishing, 2005)

happy! It contains the amino acid tyrosine, which helps make us feel content, while the fats in cheese encourage the brain to make dopamine - the feel-good hormone.[19]

Additionally, remember that soft cheeses are believed to have an extra benefit of being good for the gut as the surviving lactic acid bacteria are considered probiotic. People who include cheese, especially 'live' cheese, into their daily diets get essential nutrients, vitamins and minerals, which encourage strong teeth, healthy muscles and hair, and smooth skin. Most importantly, these people can enjoy having a healthy digestive tract, healthy metabolism and, as a result, a good mood.

The real key to a healthy body and mind is balance and moderation. It would be unhealthy to consume a kilo of fine cheese in one sitting to 'maximise' the health benefits and I do not believe anyone in the world has ever done it. To enjoy good health and happiness it is important to eat fine cheese regularly, slowly and in moderation - not too much, but not too little.

The secret to moderation

I know, I know. Moderation sounds boring. But a lot of people forget to have moderation in moderation, too. Occasional splurges are more than welcome, which makes this whole moderation business a lot more manageable.

19   McCalman, M, *Mastering Cheese: Lessons for Connoisseurship from a Maître Fromager* (Clarkson Potter, 2009)

I'd like to introduce you to my biggest mantra and one of my wellness secrets: 'Everything in moderation. Even moderation.' Would you like to adopt this mantra too?

Most people I speak to about cheese confess that they have an issue with moderation. I honestly believe that is because they don't eat cheese *often enough*. People think moderation is not fun, but it is truly the key to your lifelong enjoyment of fine cheese, as well as to your physical and mental wellness.

I've shared my struggle with an eating disorder when I was younger. I was caught in repeating cycles of overeating and starvation. The life-changing new habit for me was having *regular* food intake. These days I'm a three-meals-a-day kind of girl. You won't catch me leaving the house without my breakfast. I'll always find time for lunch, and I definitely make sure I have a lovely slow dinner with my family. There are also regular treats dotted throughout my days and weeks - chocolate, cheese, ice cream. But there is one important caveat - my nourishment has to be of as high quality as possible. High quality to me means natural food that is developed without hormone injections, artificial flavourings, nutrient additives and other chemical interventions.

I truly believe that the secret to moderation is avoiding extremes and opting for *quality over quantity*. When you ban cheese, chocolate or ice cream - in other words, little treats - from your diet, suddenly, it's all you can think about. On the other hand, when nothing is banned and all delicious foods are just a normal part of your life you won't obsess about them anymore or overindulge. I encourage you to have little treats regularly and make them a normal part of your diet and life. If you'd like to have a little cheeseboard with your partner or friends, feel free to do it every week. Don't feel you have to wait for a big blow out at Christmas. It is important to bear in mind that all treats have to be consumed in sensible quantities and be part of a *balanced* diet.

Sensible quantities of cheese

Let's look at what constitutes sensible quantities when it comes to cheese. If you are planning to serve a cheeseboard after a nutritionally balanced lunch or dinner, it is safe and good to enjoy 50-100 grams of cheese per person in total cut into bite-sized pieces. It may not seem like a lot but you will see that when you slow down and savour each morsel (which we will discuss in Chapter 6 in more detail), you will get as much pleasure as if you were to consume much bigger amounts mindlessly.

For me, a sure way to overindulge in cheese is not to eat it often enough. If you only ever enjoy cheese for Christmas or birthdays, you are more likely to overconsume. My prescription for you is to enjoy fine cheeses *often* and in moderate quantities and you will be sure to feel happy, rewarded and balanced throughout the year. In our house, a cheeseboard is served most Saturdays. Not only it is a welcome treat at the end of a long week, but it is also a great way to re-connect, slow down and celebrate life.

My health and diet practices

I hope that what I am about to say does not come a shock but, despite being the Cheese Lady, I do not live off cheese alone. It plays a major role in my life but it represents only a small percentage of my diet and health practices, which I would like to share with you.

To ensure I continue to enjoy good physical and mental health, in addition to having great cheese throughout the year, I practise the following:

△ **Avoid medication and favour homeopathic cures instead:** I know that in some instances, drugs are crucial and unavoidable but we do not need to consume them for minor ailments that can be treated with homeopathic cures or changes in the diet.

△ **Sauna:** having grown up in Russia, I know how powerful and necessary it is to get rid of our toxins through sweating on a regular basis. Most Russians respect sauna (even more than they respect vodka), going to the sauna at least once a month or even once a week.

△ **One sweet a day:** ever since developing a healthy relationship with food, I allow myself one sweet a day. Because the number and the portion size are limited, I never waste the opportunity - I go for the best stuff. If it's ice cream, it has to be artisan; if it's chocolate, it has to be my favourite; if it's a dessert, it has to be handmade. If at all possible,

I aim to enjoy it before 2pm. That way, I'm sure it is fully burned off before I go to bed.

△ **Regular consumption of fresh fruit and vegetables:** the importance of fresh fibre in fruit and vegetables is well established. I am a firm adherent.

△ **Regular and moderate exercise:** I walk at least 8,000 steps a day and more at the weekend.

△ **Drink water regularly, instead of soft drinks:** I have not had a soft drink in over twenty years and am happy to get all my daily hydration from water. Occasionally, I squeeze a bit of lemon juice into it for extra freshness and alkalisation, which is believed to be powerful for fighting signs of ageing.

△ **Eat together with the family:** we tend to eat breakfast and dinner together for most of the week. It is the most powerful way to stay connected and balanced.

△ **Yoga and meditation:** I'm pretty new to yoga and meditation but I find that these two practices are essential in helping me unwind my busy brain, but also slow down and savour things more.

Feel free to borrow some of my practices – they are good ones. As a disclaimer I must remind you that I'm not a physician or a nutritionist, but simply a fellow human who has found a way to good health and food happiness.

Spotlight on cheese: STICHELTON

Stichelton: taste of the authentic

Nineteen eighty-nine was a tragic year for British cheese-making. It was the year when the last producer of raw milk Stilton – Colston Bassett – decided that from now on their cheese would be made only from pasteurised milk. Shortly thereafter, the requirement to make Stilton *only* from pasteurised milk became enshrined in law, thus wiping out the authentic of Stilton that for centuries prior had been made with raw milk.

In 2005 Randolph Hodgson, the founder of Neal's Yard Dairy in London, and Joe Schneider, an American cheesemaker, decided to revive the original Stilton. The only issue was that because the name of the cheese was protected by law, they couldn't call it Stilton. With some help from a member of the English Place Names Society, they discovered that an earlier name for the village of Stilton was Stichelton and thus their cheese became named. But what is so special about raw milk and does it really play an important part in the character of the cheese? Without a shadow of a doubt.

Raw milk is a whimsical substance and requires utmost respect and careful handling, but in the hands of professional artisan cheesemakers it produces outstanding cheeses that offer length and depth of flavour, superior texture and are packed with micronutrients that cannot be replicated by the pasteurised versions.

The Stichelton Dairy is based on the Welbeck Estate on the northern tip of Sherwood Forest in Nottinghamshire, where their herd of Holstein cows graze happily outdoors during the warmer months of the year, enjoying fresh grasses, herbs and flowers, ensuring the highest quality of the crucial raw ingredient.

STICHELTON
The most authentic Stilton-recipe cheese today

When I visited the Stichelton Dairy, Joe explained how refrigeration can negatively affect the microflora of milk. Therefore, they pump raw milk straight from the cows into the vat each morning. While they are letting that set, they have to regularly top stir it to prevent cream separation. Once the curd is formed, it is cut manually with a cheese harp. After draining whey, cheesemakers manually ladle freshly cut curds onto a draining trolley. This labour-intensive process is necessary to create a delicate curd.

The entire process from milk to a formed cheese takes twenty-four hours, which is considered a 'long make' in today's world. Large commercial operations can go from milk to cheese in four to six hours. But this is the key to bringing out the complexity of the milk and letting the flavour grow and develop over time.

Stichelton has a more profound flavour than today's Stiltons without being too aggressive. Wonderfully buttery, nutty and sometimes even chocolatey, it impresses me with its rich mouth-coating texture, especially when matured for over five or six months. It is worth bearing in mind that this farmhouse cheese is directly related to how the milk behaved when it was made so it will inevitably vary from day to day, from month to month, from season to season. Do not expect it to be the same every time you get to enjoy it, but rather embrace its wonderful variability. Having said that, my absolute favourite time to have Stichelton is from November to February.

How to enjoy Stichelton

Much like the famous Stilton/port duo, Stichelton will pair beautifully with port, especially the Reserve variety of Tawny, Ruby or Vintage ports. Other dessert and fortified wines with deep nutty, caramelly and spicy notes - such as Banyuls or Oloroso and Palo Cortado sherries - will compliment it nicely too.

SUMMARY

In this chapter, we have dealt with the important subject of balancing a healthy diet with enjoying quality cheese and learned that the key to continuous enjoyment is moderation and quality. We've covered the nutritional composition of cheese to develop your understanding of the health benefits to be gained from its consumption. Finally, I've given you my own personal tips to keep healthy in body and soul.

In our next chapter we will move onto Step 4, which is about developing your conscious appreciation skills and as a result getting more pleasure out of every morsel of cheese you have.

CHAPTER 6

Step 4: Conscious Appreciation

One of the keys to getting the full benefit of anything, be it a piece of fine art, a holiday or a walk, is doing it while fully engaging your consciousness. A holiday has no benefit if your mind is not there and all you are thinking about is work. When you are physically present, but your mind is not, then you may as well not be there physically. Enjoying fine cheese is no exception. In this chapter, you will learn the art of slowing down and savouring cheese. Only when you master the art of consciously and deliberately savouring fine cheese with your palate and your mind can you begin to appreciate the true pleasures of it. There are several elements to enjoying farmhouse and artisan cheese consciously.

Being present

When enjoying fine cheese, your mind needs to be completely focused on the experience that is unfolding. One simply cannot savour cheese fully on autopilot.

It takes practice, just like other mindful activities such as yoga and meditation, but the benefits are noticeable and absolutely worth the effort. True appreciation, understanding and enjoyment of fine cheese happen when your mind is not distracted by outside 'noise'. As fun as it is to share cheeseboards with your friends and family, you don't generally get to appreciate the complexity and uniqueness of aroma, flavour and texture. During lovely get-togethers, our minds are so focused on the conversation that we tend to mindlessly pop delicious things into our mouths, forgetting to experience them. Delicacies become just calories.

I would like to encourage you (at least occasionally) to spend some *quality time* with your fine cheeses alone (or accompanied by just one like-minded person). Once you master savouring cheese alone you will be able to do it in larger groups of people. You just need to rewire your brain to pay attention to certain things and, once the connections are there, it will become second nature.

How to taste cheese properly

It is important to take time to taste cheese properly. Here are some pointers:

- △ Prepare your environment. It should have good natural light and be free of odours, noise and distraction.

- △ Prepare your palate. It should be free of strong lingering flavours, smoke or alcohol.

- △ Always taste cheeses at room temperature (take them out of the fridge at least 30 minutes before tasting).

- △ Taste lighter cheeses first, strong ones last.

- △ Use your five senses.

The first four points are self-explanatory. I'd like to delve into the last one and explore it in more detail.

The five senses

As humans, we all have five senses: hearing, sight, touch, smell, taste. Not all of us remember to engage each of the senses in equal measure when we have new experiences or try new foods.

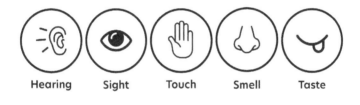

Hearing   Sight   Touch   Smell   Taste

The five senses

To fully experience fine cheese, you need to use all five senses.

Hearing

When cutting and preparing your cheese, pay attention to what you can hear and what that tells you. Are you starting to get excited when you hear the rustling of cheese paper? Is the cheese making any noises that can give you clues to how it will be on the palate?

Sight

Start by examining how the cheese looks. Do not rush. See what colour the paste and the rind are. If it is yellow, what kind of yellow - hay, golden, cream? What does the texture look like? Is it gooey or firm? Crumbly or smooth? Are there crystals in the paste? The appearance will give you clues as to what milk the cheese is made from, and what its texture, age and even flavour intensity are.

Touch

It may seem odd, but poke at your cheese. If a seemingly firm cheese yields under your finger and bounces back when you remove the pressure, I would describe this cheese as semi-firm. If a firm cheese yields with touch but only slightly, the cheese is firm in texture. If a cheese is solid as a rock and there is absolutely no yield under pressure, the cheese is hard. Needless to say, soft cheeses will stick to your finger and feel creamy in consistency.

Smell

Farmhouse and artisan cheeses have a wonderful aroma, which is definitely a big part of the savouring experience. The complexity of aroma accounts for much of the difference between basic and fine cheese. Make sure to take in the amazing aromas. Smell the paste and the rind. To get a burst of aromas from a cheese that has been aerated while coming to room temperature, break its paste right under your nose and take a deep inhale. What do you smell? Do the sweet or savoury notes prevail? Is it fruity or nutty? Or maybe a bit farmyardy? Think of other foods these smells remind you of. Take notes, even if they are only mental ones.

Taste

This is the most desired part of the whole process. Notice how the gooey-looking cheese envelops your palate in creaminess. Notice if the flavours match the smell. Do not rush to swallow. Take care to chew each morsel mindfully, paying close attention to the flavour and texture. What flavours can you recognise? Does the taste remind you of other foods or anything else?

To take your taste experience even further, consider the following:

△ **Initial impression:** pay attention to what you perceive the second a morsel touches your tongue to discover the most basic flavours.

△ **Mid-chew:** work your cheese into a mushy substance with the aid of your saliva and taste the new flavours that unfold.

△ **Aftertaste:** savour and luxuriate in the afterglow that a particularly good cheese leaves in your mouth. The finer the cheese, the longer the flavour.

Having your first proper cheese tasting experience can feel like a lot of work and you may be stuck for words to describe the smell and taste sensations. Worry not, it will get easier with practice.

Flavours and aromas of cheese

The great news is that most of us are great at distinguishing the primary flavours of cheese. The *primary flavours* are sweet, savoury (umami), acidic, salty, and bitter. On the other hand, the situation with the more complex flavours and aromas, such as nutty, herbaceous and meaty, is a bit trickier. For the purposes of this book, we'll call them *secondary flavours*. Many people have confessed to me that they find it overwhelming and confusing when it comes to pinpointing these complex flavours. There is no real shortcut to getting good at distinguishing the secondary flavours and aromas, other than tasting cheeses frequently (especially comparatively) and taking notes.

The table below contains a useful list of secondary cheese flavours that you can always refer back to when you are sampling new cheeses, and it is a great vocabulary starting point for beginners for describing your fine cheeses without getting too bogged down with the trade jargon.

The most common secondary cheese flavours and aromas

Fruity	Mushroom	Rich	Buttery
Creamy	Eggy	Nutty	Butterscotch
Fudge	Chocolate	Toasty	Meaty
Beefy	Spicy	Powerful	Tart
Herbaceous	Stinky	Pungent	Farmyard
Smoky	Earthy	Musty	Mouldy
Malt	Broth	Yoghurt	Lactic
Sharp	Aromatic	Savoury	Biting
Aged	Zesty	Lemony	Tropical
Sour	Acidic	Potato	Zingy

But the list is by no means exhaustive. When you are in the process of savouring a cheese, and it reminds you of your grandma's jam or that scrumptious ham you had in Italy, that is absolutely fine. Just say that it was jammy or hammy. The beautiful thing is that there is no right or wrong answer. Everyone's perception of taste and their flavour memory are completely unique.

If, like me, you are quite studious, you can keep written notes on all the cheese you taste. When I started my cheese career, I used to keep a diary, where I described the texture, flavour and aroma of each new cheese I sampled. I found that writing things down made me slow down, pay attention and be more inquisitive about the new flavours. After 168 entries in the diary, it became second nature to taste cheese properly using all five senses without having to write notes.

Initial principles of pairing cheese

In this section we will be talking mostly about pairing cheeses with wine, but you can use the same principles for pairing cheese with other popular alcoholic beverages such as beer, cider, whisky and gin, as well as non-alcoholic ones, such as tea and coffee.

The terms *matching* and *pairing* are often used interchangeably but the two have somewhat different meanings. *Pairing* a food with a beverage means finding *complementary* flavours in them (think of salty foods paired with sweet wines for balance), whereas *matching* a particular food to a drink means finding *the same* descriptive elements in both of them (think of matching a fruity cheese and a fruity drink).

There are some rules that you may hear about when it comes to matching and pairing cheeses with beverages and we'll look at some of them below. But the most important thing I'd like you to bear in mind is that finding the best combinations can be incredibly subjective. Your palate and your taste preferences are the ones that *really* matter when enjoying cheeses and wines at home. Remember, there is no such thing as the 'cheese police' who will arrive to check on you to see if you're doing something wrong. The most important principle of any indulgent experience at home is that you enjoy it, not that you follow all the rules.

However, if you have no idea where to start with your cheese and wine pairings/matches at home, let's briefly look at some common notions and see if they have any merit, and then we'll look at some key principles for finding good flavour combinations of your own.

You may have heard the following statements when it comes to cheese and wine pairing. I believe them to be largely true and they are a great starting point for finding good flavour combinations.

△ **What grows together goes together:** this is especially true in the Old World. For instance, goat's milk cheeses and white wines made in the Loire Valley are simply made for each other.

△ **Cheese and wine should have the same intensity:** it is true because if you have a young cheese, let's say mozzarella, for example, with a full-bodied complex red wine, the cheese will be lost and overshadowed by the wine.

The following notion, however, has outlived its usefulness.

△ **Cheese should always be served only with red wine:** this view used to be strongly held, but thankfully the world has evolved and we can now enjoy fine cheese with white, rosé and sparkling wines, and even beer, whisky and gin. The variety of flavours and aromas within the fine cheese universe is incredible and it needs the whole spectrum of drinks to match it.

The main aim in pairing/matching cheeses and wines is harmony. The interaction between cheese and its accompanying beverage should be smooth and agreeable, especially flavour-wise. They should enhance each other without conflicting or overpowering. Ideally, your cheese and drink combination will produce a 'third flavour' and become bigger than the sum of its parts.

I would describe the possible outcomes of combining cheeses and wines by giving the pairings one of these three names:

△ **Foes:** your cheese and wine clash and make each other worse than they are separately. They cannot and will never agree on your palate. It's a bad combination.

△ **Friends:** your cheese and wine work nicely together on your palate but they do not become bigger than the sum of their parts. It's a good combination.

△ **Lovers:** your cheese and wine blend on your palate in perfect harmony, creating a flavour that neither one of them had separately. They create a 'third flavour' and become bigger than the sum of their parts. It's an outstanding combination.

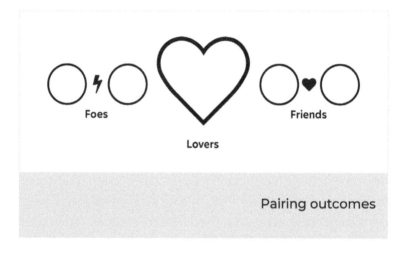

Foes

Friends

Lovers

Pairing outcomes

Most pairings and matches will fall into the 'Friends' or even 'Best friends' category. 'Lovers' combinations do exist (for me, it's the classic Roquefort and Sauternes pairing) but they are extremely rare.

How to pair cheese and wine

Primary flavours

The first step to finding good and even outstanding combi-nations is focusing on primary flavours and understanding how they will interact. The Wine and Spirits Educations Trust (WSET), a global wine educational organisation, provides a useful guide on these interactions, which I have adapted to use for cheese.[20] Read through the expected flavour interaction below and refer to them when contem-plating your next pairing/matching experience.

For instance, if your cheese is primarily sweet, bear in mind that it can increase bitterness, acidity and burn. That's not something that anyone would want so avoid choosing wines that are already high in those primary flavours.

Just to remind you, the primary flavours in cheese can be:

- △ Sweetness

- △ Umami

- △ Acidity

- △ Salt

- △ Bitterness

---

20   WSET, *Wines and Spirits: Understanding Style and Quality* (WSET, 2012)

If your cheese's primary flavour is sweetness, it can:

△ Increase bitterness, acidity, astringency and burn

△ Decrease body, richness, sweetness and fruit

The good news is that extreme sweetness is virtually non-existent in the cheese world, since most cheeses contain perceptible amounts of salt. However, it's good to bear in mind that moderately sweet cheeses such as ricotta and gouda can make a bitter wine more bitter or a thin wine even thinner.

If your cheese's primary flavour is umami, it can:

△ Increase bitterness, acidity, astringency, burn

△ Decrease body, richness, fruitiness and sweetness

Very ripe soft cheeses are known to have umami compounds so, when planning to enjoy your ripe Brie de Meaux or Camembert de Normandie, consider the levels of bitterness, astringency and acidity in your wine and try to avoid wines that are naturally high in those primary flavours. Sometimes with ripe gooey cheeses you just have to think outside the box and go with a cider instead.

If your cheese is high in acidity, it can:

△ Increase richness, fruitiness and sweetness

△ Decrease acidity

Fresh and young cheese such as fresh goat's curd and

chèvres from the Loire Valley can have a positive impact on wine with lively and high acidity and light body. They make naturally light and highly zesty wines sing with their range of fruit and floral notes. Don't take this balancing act too far. If the wine is already balanced in acidity and sweetness, adding zingy cheeses would only throw it out of balance.

If your cheese's primary flavour is salt, it can:

△ Decrease bitterness, astringency, burn and acidity

△ Increase richness and smoothness

This is what every cheese fan loves to hear – that their favourite food will make their wine less bitter and astringent, while increasing its richness and smoothness. Bear in mind that salt levels in cheese vary according to type and age. The majority of cheeses do contain perceptible amounts of salt. Remember to factor in the texture and maturity of your cheese.

If your cheese is high in bitterness, it can:

△ Increase bitterness

Bitterness is not something that cheese is famous for. However, there are certain styles of cheese, like the thistle rennet cheeses of Western Spain and Portugal, which have that signature trait. They are notoriously difficult to pair with wine. Whatever you do, do not pick wine that is naturally bitter.

TOMME DE SAVOIE
A classic cheese from the French Alps

Secondary flavours

The second step you can take to pair or match your cheese and wine is to harmonise them based on their secondary flavours. A good match would be to go for a fruity cheese (nine-month-old Appenzeller Edel, for example) and a fruity red wine such as Merlot. This is an example of both the cheese and the wine having the same secondary flavour. For a pairing you could try a buttery and toasty champagne with a nutty Gruyère. The secondary flavours are obviously different, but they are *complementary*.

Intensity and body

Fine cheeses not only have different flavours and aromas, but they may also vary significantly in *intensity* (the strength of flavour) and *body* (the weight on the palate). Being able to identify these aspects correctly can help you find good cheese and wine combinations.

The most useful and straightforward way to describe the intensity and body is to use these terms:

△ Light

△ Medium

△ Full

If you'd like to vary your cheese vocabulary, I'd like to also suggest using the following descriptive terms.

Intensity and body descriptors

Bold	Powerful	Complex
Delicate	Lingering	Pervasive
Light	Elegant	Heavy

As a rule of thumb, it's good to remember that intensity is most likely to increase with age. The more mature the cheese is, the more likely it will require an intense wine to match.

When it comes to body, it is not always as straightforward. In most cases, more mature and firmer cheeses will have a fuller body and will require a full-bodied wine. However, there are relatively young cheeses, such as triple crèmes (such as Brillat Savarin and Délice des Crémiers) that have a rich body but pair nicely with light to medium wines, such as champagne.

Do it your way

If all of the above sounds like a lot of hard work, I recommend just doing it your way and finding out what works through experimentation.

Take a morsel of cheese and break it into fine mush in your mouth. Pay close attention to the flavour sensations. Without swallowing, add a small amount of wine to the mush and close your eyes for better focus.

Ask yourself: how is the flavour of cheese interacting with the wine? Do they work *together*? Is one overwhelming the other? Is one bringing any unpleasant qualities in the other? Do they create a good blend that is enjoyable? Or do they even become bigger than the sum of their parts?

If the combination is good, you'll have a positive answer to the questions above. If you answer yes to the final question, congratulations! You have hit the wine and cheese jackpot - you've discovered an outstanding pairing.

The principles and techniques in this section of the book should provide a good guide for exploring the exciting world of fine cheese and wine pairings. Let's have a look at what other things you can pair cheeses with.

Cheese and honey

Good cheeses and honeys are delicious and good for you separately but are even more amazing when enjoyed together. Here in Britain, pairing cheese and honey may seem unusual, but in France, Italy and Greece, people have enjoyed them together for centuries.

The cheese/honey duo is appropriate at any time of the day. If you want to enjoy them for breakfast then the most appropriate cheeses would be young, creamy, milky ones, like ricotta, cottage cheese and even burrata. Drizzled with runny honey, they gain another beautiful dimension, as well as a whole lot of health-enriching properties.

During the day, you can go for slightly more mature and more intense flavoured cheeses like La Tur, Selles-sur-Cher and even Gorgonzola Dolce. On a light cracker with a drizzle or a scoop of honey, they will be a gorgeous treat after a leisurely brunch or lunch. If you prefer harder cheese, like Pecorino or cheddar, I recommend opting for set honey, like Scottish heather honey.

In the evening I would suggest serving your big hitters, especially if the cheeseboard is the last course of the meal. Big-flavoured cheeses like Isle of Mull, Fiore Sardo or extra mature Comté, as well as strong blues like Roquefort and Stilton, all pair with honey nicely. The intense sweetness of honey mellows out the big character of the cheese and creates a match made in heaven. Either runny or set honey will work beautifully.

What are the crunchy bits?

As you develop your skill of conscious appreciation of farmhouse and artisan cheese, you'll start noticing more about the textures of various cheeses. One of the things that is sure to grab your attention is the little white bits, also known as crystals, in the paste of some cheese.

The main variety of crystals are *tyrosine crystals*. They are a result of protein breakdown during maturation, when cheeses evolve not only in flavour but also in their chemical composition. The longer the ageing process lasts, the more the proteins within the cheese break down into tyrosine amino acids. They then tend to clump together and form bright white crystals. The more mature the cheese is, the bigger the crystals will be. At the same time, these cheeses naturally taste saltier because of flavour concentration through moisture loss during ageing. For example, extra mature cheddar will taste saltier than a young one and it will have crystals.

The second variety of crystals you may find in cheese is calcium lactate. This variety is not nearly as prevalent but can appear on the outside and inside of the cheese and tends to be paler and less crunchy. Calcium lactate crystals are more prevalent on cheddar-style cheeses.

The two crystal varieties can appear alongside each other – for instance, in aged goudas and Parmigiano Reggiano. The best way to tell two varieties of crystals apart is to do a lot of comparative research and tasting.

Spotlight on cheese: CORRA LINN

Corra Linn: the bonniest cheese

Having lived in Scotland for over a decade now, I consider this bonny country my second home. Not only do I enjoy its stunning countryside, coastlines and wonderful castles, I love visiting our best cheesemakers. Errington Cheese, the producer of Corra Linn, has a special place in my heart. The farm is located in South Lanarkshire at the foot of the Pentland Hills. It's only 25 miles from Edinburgh but it could be a whole world away, with its slower and quieter pace of life.

When I first visited the farm over a decade ago, the original founder, Humphrey Errington, was still at the helm. At the end of our private tour, Humphrey invited my friend and I to sample the newest cheese he was working on. It was a nameless cheddar-style ewe's milk cheese – the predecessor to today's Corra Linn.

Over the years, the recipe has improved and been perfected, and it is now an outstanding cheese that I am proud to sell in my shop. Made from the raw milk of 300 Lacaune ewes that reside on the farm, and matured for a minimum of twelve months, it is similar to any good traditional cheddar, but with a lot more nuttiness and pleasant sweetness on the palate. It is worth seeking out Corra Linn that's been matured for over eighteen months because that is when its complexity and nuance shine through even brighter.

Today, the cheesemaking business is run by Humphrey's daughter Selina and her family. They are doing incredible things on the cheesemaking scene in Scotland. In the last couple of years, they have significantly expanded their range. Their flagship ewe's milk cheese, Lanark Blue, is now joined by a cohort of goat's milk cheeses made from their new flock of dairy goats (a mixture of Saanen, Toggenburg and Alpine). I especially love their Biggar Blue, Tinto, Bonnington Linn and Blackmount.

How to enjoy Corra Linn

When pairing Corra Linn with beverages, I tend to go for medium-bodied red wines to match its complex flavour and weight, but nice craft ales with a bit of sweetness and nuttiness on the palate will make a great match for it too.

SUMMARY

In this chapter, we have looked in depth at the key ways to bring conscious appreciation into enjoying fine cheese, which is Step 4 to achieving cheese happiness. We've looked at how to engage all of the five senses when tasting cheese, how to describe the cheeses you taste and finally, once you have selected your favourite cheeses, what wines to combine your cheese with.

In the next chapter, we will cover the final step in the Cheese Connoisseur's Way to cheese happiness, which is how to connect and celebrate around cheese with friends and family.

CHAPTER 7

Step 5: Connection

British society today is the product of its remarkable history. Over the centuries, this country developed at a speed matched only by a handful of other countries. But the first-world-country status that we enjoy today also has its downsides. Among them is an epidemic of stress and anxiety. The results of the Mental Health Foundation's study in 2018 tell us that 74% of people felt so stressed in the previous year that they were overwhelmed or unable to cope.[21] There are numerous causes of this epidemic but one could be our loss of the strong social bonds and connections that used to define our societies up until a few decades ago.

Paradoxically, we have more connections today than ever before, but these connections are of a superficial and virtual nature. It is impossible to keep in touch and care about thousands of 'friends' on Facebook in equal measure. To reverse this trend, we should focus on the quality of our real life social connections, not the number.

I know a thing or two about the power of deep social connections. Having been born and raised in Russia of

---

21   Mental Health Foundation, 'Stressed Nation: 74% of UK "overwhelmed or unable to cope" at some point in the past year' (2018), www.mentalhealth.org.uk/news/stressed-nation-74-uk-overwhelmed-or-unable-cope-some-point-past-year, accessed April 2021

the Soviet era, where people suffered economically, all we had was each other and our communities. Family meals and celebrations were the glue that held us all together and kept our spirits up. When you cannot buy even basic things, you start treasuring the free things in life, such as each other's company. That's why, in this chapter, I'd like to talk about the importance of Step 7 - Connection - and inspire you to rekindle this simple pleasure and essential ingredient of a good life.

But how do we strengthen those social bonds and connections?

The first practice we need to re-adopt is to break bread together. Regularly. At the table. Over conversation. With no television or screens present. As basic as it may seem, I know it works.

Nourishing human connections

The case is clear - we need to slow down and eat together on a regular basis. The faster our lives get, the less time we spend at the table. Some people literally eat on the run. It is important to start thinking about our meals as an investment in our overall wellbeing, and building them into the fabric of our lives on a consistent basis. The majority of our meals should be enjoyed with other humans. We need to recognise that food is not merely fuel and building blocks for our body cells, it is also nourishment for our souls, which get super-charged when we eat together. Simple conversations about everyday things are fundamental to forming stronger connections between us. The more we share the seemingly mundane things with each other, the more we bond.

Most of us already know that slow breakfasts and leisurely dinners with family are amazing for strengthening connections, and meals with friends are a source of energy and inspiration. What we tend to forget is that it doesn't have to be fancy. A simple dish, prepared at home in a relaxed atmosphere, be it a frittata or a quiche, can trump lobster thermidor when enjoyed in the company of your nearest and dearest. It is the simple things in life that really matter and that bring us closer together. If we look to our favourite European holiday destinations, namely Italy, France and Greece, we can admire the leisurely pace of life in these countries. People there understand the power of a slow family meal and are known to have strong social bonds. Let's take that inspiration and ingrain it into our lives.

Often, when a meal is over, it is the cheeseboard that features on the table. It has a magical ability to keep everyone around for longer. The best and most relaxed conversations happen over a cheeseboard. You wouldn't and you shouldn't have a cheeseboard every day, out of health considerations. However, it is completely possible to have a mini cheese treat every Friday or Saturday. It is a tradition in our house to prepare a cheeseboard or plate just for the two of us, when the little one is finally tucked up in bed, and to slow down, sampling and savouring the cheeses and discussing what we are tasting, with a little glass of wine, of course.

Little celebrations

There is another silent killer operating in our society and that is our obsession with always wanting that new shiny thing. A lot of us fall into this trap and we forget to celebrate what we already have, celebrating little things. Life should be made up of little celebrations. Marking wins, accomplishments, milestones or just a nice day should be woven into the fabric of our daily lives. It is too easy to get caught up in the never-ending sea of work, struggles and never being quite there yet. Of course, not everyone can afford a meal in a Michelin-starred restaurant to mark significant occasions. A celebration is a little treat for the soul. For foodies like me, it can come in the shape of a fabulous pastry or cake, scrumptious artisan ice cream, a complex and lingering glass of champagne or other fine wine or, of course, some gloriously complex fine cheese. The trick to making these mini treats count is to have them regularly and mindfully. We should have a little celebratory treat every day (or at least every week).

If you decide your celebratory treat is going to be some fine cheese and wine, I would like to suggest a few combinations that will set your soul singing and make your stress melt away:

- △ Burrata with chestnut honey and a glass of prosecco

- △ Délice des Crémiers with a glass of champagne

- △ Baked Vacherin Mont d'Or with a simple red or white wine

△   Roquefort with Sauternes

△   Stichelton with Vintage Port

The art of a cheeseboard

A full cheeseboard is the ultimate treat for any cheese aficionado. I also believe that a cheeseboard is an amazing vehicle for creating connection. Just think of the times when you lingered over some cheese and conversation at the end of a meal. A cheeseboard makes us slow down and enjoy each other's company.

There are no hard and fast rules when it comes to composing a cheeseboard (remember, there's no such thing as the cheese police), but I'd like to offer you some guidelines to enhance your enjoyment, raise your cheese game and impress your friends and family:

△   Include a variety of milks, styles and ages (refer to the different varieties in Chapter 3).

△   Include at least four to five cheeses, as there is more scope to showcase different styles. Three cheeses can make up a cheeseboard for a small group of people, but there is less scope for variety.

△   Arrange the cheeses from mild to strong, which generally means start with the soft and finish with the blue.

△   Ideally, choose a beverage that most, if not all, the cheeses on the board will pair with. For instance, create a cheeseboard for a particular red or white wine. Alternatively, your cheeseboard can feature 'versatile' cheeses that can go with any wine regardless of the colour. If in doubt, ask your cheesemonger for advice.

In case you would like more specific ideas around creating a fantastic cheeseboard, I've created a few formulae you can follow to make the process a bit easier. They come with specific cheese examples too to serve as a baseline you can build on.

Soft + semi-firm + firm/hard + blue

△ Brie de Meaux + Rachel + Fiore Sardo + Blue des Causses

Bloomy rind + washed rind + natural rind + blue

△ Baron Bigod + Morbier + Etivaz + Roquefort

Semi-firm & crumbly + firm & smooth + soft & blue

△ Gorwydd Caerphilly + Ossau Iraty + Gorgonzola Dolce

For seasonal cheeseboard ideas, please visit the Resource section at the end of the book.

What about condiments?

I've heard from some of my customers that in the 1970s cheeseboards were especially fashionable and it was common practice to serve the cheeses with some grapes, celery and plain biscuits. It seems this fashion hasn't changed much and the majority of British people still opt for this classic condiment combination.

There is nothing wrong with this preference but if you'd like to vary your condiment game, it's worth thinking a bit more broadly. Condiments are a matter of personal taste so there won't be a 'one-size-fits-all' solution. It's worth experimenting and finding the combinations that work for you.

Broadly speaking, if you're serving a cheeseboard with a variety of styles and flavours, my recommendation is to opt for neutral crisp crackers (think Bath ovals) or a baguette, which will not overpower any of the cheeses and will serve as a useful palate-cleanser between the flavours. The better the quality of your crackers, the more sophisticated and delicious the experience will be, so I would urge you not to skimp on the crackers but to go for the good (artisan) stuff. Being a bit of cheese purist, I tend to not have my cheese *on* a cracker. Instead, I use crackers as a palate-cleanser between my cheese bites, but it is a matter of personal preference so whatever works for you is the way to go.

In Scotland, we are spoiled for choice when it comes to the variety of oatcakes – they come in all shapes, sizes and thicknesses. I love oatcakes, but for me they work only with certain varieties of cheese, mostly firm British cheeses, for instance Isle of Mull cheddar, Dunlop and Caerphilly.

Quince paste (also known as membrillo) is a superb condiment that can work across the board with most cheeses, so if you are ever in doubt, go for this classic condiment. Other accompaniments, such as flavoured crackers, chutneys, fresh and dried fruits and nuts, may be chosen based on whether they match or contrast with the flavour of the cheese. For instance, the nutty flavour of Comté can be matched by walnuts, whereas a salty Pecorino can be complimented by the opposite sweetness of honey.

You can find more condiment recommendations for each cheese style back in Chapter 3.

How much per person?

While it is nearly impossible to give a definitive answer applicable to every group of people and every dining situation, there are some strategies.

Cheeseboard for four to ten people

If you're planning to serve a cheeseboard at your dinner party, arrange 250-400 gram wedges on a board and cut at least one slice off each cheese to show how they should be cut. Place a medium-sized knife next to every cheese as this will help to avoid cross-contamination of flavours. A nice versatile cheeseboard would include four to five different styles varying in texture, flavour, milk and aroma. For examples of nicely balanced cheeseboards, refer to my recommendation earlier in this chapter.

Individually plated cheese course

If you intend to serve individual cheese plates with four to five cheeses, allow 30 grams of each cheese per person. Remember to opt for a variety of styles to give your guests a fuller and more exciting dining experience and arrange the cheeses in a clock-like fashion starting with a milder one at 'twelve o'clock' and finishing with the strongest one at 'ten/eleven o'clock'.

Small celebration cheeseboard for two

A small cheeseboard is a great way to slow down and savour life with your other half. It can be enjoyed every week so the key is not to overindulge at any one time. I recommend using three to five cheeses and cutting them into small wedges or even cubes, which will help you to enjoy them slowly and mindfully. In total, 40–100 grams of cheese per person is a good amount you can enjoy every week.

How to serve

Farmhouse and artisan cheeses taste best at room temperature when their flavours are 'open'. Take your cheeses out of the fridge at least 30 minutes or even an hour before they will be served. Cut as much as you will need off the wedge and put the rest back in the fridge. Arrange the cut pieces/wedges on your chosen board, slate or plate and cover with a cloche so that cheeses can come to room temperature *without drying out*. This will prevent them from losing their aroma and, as a result, flavour to the elements. In the absence of a pretty cloche, cover your cheeseboard loosely with a wax wrap or foil.

When to serve

When planning a cheeseboard, consider the time of day it is going to be enjoyed. Lunchtime cheeses should be a bit lighter on flavour and aroma than their night-time counterparts. You also may choose to serve cheese before or after the meal. If you feel that you never get to fully enjoy the cheese course because you are just too full after a meal, it is completely acceptable to serve it as an appetiser, especially at a function with finger foods. Young and creamy cheeses will be perfect as they will beautifully match light and sparkling pre-dinner wines. I especially recommend burrata, La Tur, Délice des Crémiers and young goat's milk cheeses. However, if you are serving red wine throughout, you may want to opt for firmer cheeses such as semi-mature Pecorino, Gruyère, Comté, or even farmhouse cheddar.

Beverage selection

The after-dinner cheese selection should be dictated by the wine you're planning to have with it. Putting in a little bit of thought and planning will pay huge dividends here. The correct wine combination will elevate your whole savouring experience. When deciding on the wine, first consider its intensity and then its texture and weight. Not everyone will have a professional wine education so it is completely acceptable to use the blurb on the label to guide you. If the wine is described as a 'light' wine, it will be more appropriate for lighter, younger cheese, in contrast to the wines that are labelled 'full-bodied' or 'complex', which will require a more mature and sophisticated cheese.

Meals to include fine cheese

Some cheese lovers assume that fine cheese can only be enjoyed in the evening after a meal. While I tend to leave the strong, assertive and extra mature cheeses like sharp cheddars and blues until the end of a meal, it is possible to serve fine cheeses for breakfast, lunch and dinner. You have to balance the strength of the cheese with the time of the day.

For breakfast, light creamy cheeses such as burrata or fresh goat's curd would be most appropriate. For lunch, we can go for the medium-intensity cheeses, for example, Appenzeller, La Tur or Taleggio. As an appetiser for dinner, try stronger cheeses that are slightly saltier as they will help to whet the appetite. I'd suggest Pecorino Sardo, Manchego or Brie de Meaux.

Cheese for dinner

Melted cheese has been bringing people together for centuries. Cheese fondue is an incredible thing but getting it right can be a tricky process. You have to source the right kind of cheese, grate it, stir it and hope it amalgamates. For a relaxed and stress-free evening, I suggest using Vacherin Mont d'Or to make a super easy one-cheese fondue, instead.

Vacherin Mont d'Or is an incredible gooey treat of a cheese that every aficionado the world over patiently awaits all summer. It is in season between September and March and the wait for it makes it even more special and desirable. Mont d'Or is made from raw cow's milk and is camembert-like in texture, with a slight pungency on the rind and spruce bark around it. When this cheese is baked, it is elevated to a new level of deliciousness. Of course, it tastes even better when shared with your favourite people, possibly accompanied by a glass or two of your favourite wine.

The heart-warming one-cheese fondue is incredibly easy to prepare. Follow the steps below to bake it at home:

1. Preheat the oven to 220°C.

2. Remove plastic packaging but leave everything else as is (the cheese in the wooden box and its lid underneath).

3. Wrap the wooden box in a piece of foil.

4. Put in the oven for 25 minutes.

5. After 25 minutes, check the cheese with a spoon: if it's runny and liquid, it's nearly ready.

6. Leave the foil open and put the cheese back in the oven for 5 minutes to slightly brown the top.

Et voilà!

The best way to enjoy this gooey and wonderfully sprucy cheese is by pouring it over boiled baby potatoes and complementing it with crunchy gherkins, charcuterie and a glass of medium-bodied red (or white) wine.

How to cut fine cheese

The right way to cut cheese will ensure that every person enjoys the complexity of each cheese's texture and flavour. The wrong way will present people with diverging experiences. We know that fine cheeses come in a myriad of shapes and sizes, so when cutting individual portions of cheese from a large wedge, keep in mind the paste-to-rind ratio. Ideally, each portion should have a good amount of paste and only a bit of rind/the part nearest the rind, so that no one portion ends up with all the rind. It is especially important because, as a general rule, cheeses taste stronger closer to the rind and milder towards the centre of the wheel. Below is a visual guide to cutting common cheese varieties.

SMALL ROUND CHEESE
(Camembert de Normandie,
Epoisses, Livarot)

LARGE ROUND CHEESE
(Brie de Meaux, Baron Bigod)

SLICE OF SMALL WHEELS
(Manchego, Ossau Iraty,
Roquefort)

SLICE OF LARGE WHEELS
(Comté, Beaufort)

How to cut cheese

Spotlight on cheese:
GORWYDD CAERPHILLY

Gorwydd Caerphilly: a slice of history

Caerphilly cheese is deeply rooted in Welsh history and food culture. Prior to the mid-nineteenth century, it used to be a staple food for farmworkers and miners, but its production sharply declined to the point of extinction. Luckily for us, the farmhouse Caerphilly recipe was adopted by cheesemakers in Somerset who recognised the importance of having a quicker maturing cheese in their repertoire, while they waited for their large cheddar truckles to mature. Chris Duckett's aged Caerphilly has been keeping the high standard of real Caerphilly alive for decades.

My favourite Caerphilly is the one made by Todd and Maugan Trethowan. Todd trained with Chris Duckett in Somerset before moving to Wales and setting up production on his parents' farm using milk sourced from nearby farms. In 2014, a partnership opportunity with Puxton Farm came up and they moved back to Somerset, where they created a purpose-built dairy and maturing facility attached to the Puxton Farm Park, which boasted a herd of organically reared Holstein and Jersey cows.

When we visited, the head cheesemaker explained the benefits of being so close to the milk source as their milk has to travel only a few metres from the milking parlour to the cheesemaking vat. As a result, they don't have to pasteurise it and can keep it in a naturally beautiful state ready for cheesemaking.

GORWYDD CAERPHILLY
Traditional Welsh cheese made with raw cow's milk

The entire process, except for the milk stirring, is performed by hand. When I close my eyes, I can still see the enchanting 'dance' the four cheesemakers performed with their knives as they were texturing the curd. It was precise, well timed and careful. It gave me a new level of appreciation for the phrase 'handmade' cheese.

Another thing I learned during my visit was an invisible but fascinating part of Gorwydd Caerphilly's history. The Trethowan brothers played a pivotal role in saving a 'heritage' starter culture that was days away from extinction. With the advance of commercial cheesemaking, starter cultures have become mass-produced too, so cheeses started losing their 'taste of place'. Only a small handful of producers were still using starter cultures native to Britain.

The Trethowan brothers saved and replicated the unique culture, which is used to this day in production of their Caerphilly, ensuring its authentic taste.

Gorwydd Caerphilly is allowed to slowly mature for three to four months, which is longer than the mass-produced versions, developing a complex flavour and texture characteristic of traditional Caerphillies. I like to describe it as a cheese in three acts. Under its velvety natural rind, you'll find a cream line that's distinctly smooth, sweetly savoury and mushroomy, contrasted by its core, which is crumbly and zingy.

How to enjoy Gorwydd Caerphilly

I think this honest, unpretentious cheese is best enjoyed with some fresh crusty bread and a bowl of soup, but if you prefer to serve it on a cheeseboard, I recommend pairing it with crisp white wines or wheat beer.

SUMMARY

In this chapter, we have covered the final step of the Cheese Connoisseur's Way, which is possibly the most important. Enjoying cheese is best done as a family or among friends. We have talked about how a cheeseboard nourishes human connections and enhances the feeling of celebration around the table.

You now have the keys to creating a stunning cheeseboard – the cheese and wine to choose, the quantities to serve and how to make your cheeseboard truly memorable.

Conclusion

Now that you have reached the end of this book, I hope you feel inspired to keep exploring and learning about the wonderful and delicious world of fine cheese. Remember that cheese connoisseurship is a journey, not a destination, and that this is just the beginning.

I hope that you found the book enjoyable and insightful and it equipped you with the knowledge to become a confident cheese aficionado. Most importantly, I hope you now know how to include fine cheese in your normal diet throughout the year and savour every bite. The five steps you have learned in the Cheese Connoisseur's Way will always keep you on the right track.

They are:

1. **Cultured taste:** do not be duped by marketing tricks. Use your enquiring and logical mind to tell the difference between genuinely traditional and natural foods versus heavily marketed foods.

2. **Curated service:** choose to procure your real foods from knowledgeable purveyors who know the full story of their produce and are happy to share it with you.

3. **Continuous enjoyment:** do your best to avoid extremes, especially when it comes to what you eat. Enjoy everything in moderation throughout the year... even moderation.

4. **Conscious appreciation:** enjoy your fine cheeses, and other foods, slowly and mindfully to get more pleasure out of every bite.

5. **Connection:** make space for regular family meals. Use them to connect and celebrate the little things in life together.

I wish you all the best on your fine cheese appreciation journey!

I'm here if you ever need help. The best way to reach me is by sending an email to hello@thecheeselady.co.uk.

For cheese inspiration, tips and insights, follow me on Facebook and Instagram: @TheCheeseLadyUK

You can also subscribe to our newsletter at www.thecheese lady.co.uk/subscribe. Not only will you be the first to know about all our news, events and special offers, you will also get 10% off your first online order.

Resources

Cheeseboards by season

When composing a seasonal cheeseboard, the obvious choices may appear to be the cheeses that are fresh and made only a few days prior, like fresh goat's curd or burrata. But this view would be overly simplistic. Composing a seasonal cheeseboard is an exercise in logic and maths. You need to think back to when the cheese was born, consider if it was the best time for its production, and calculate when would be the peak for its deliciousness. Below I give you a few ideas of four seasonal cheese boards as examples of how to compose a cheeseboard that will wow your dinner guests.

The cheeseboards below are designed to offer you the crème de la crème of the fine cheese that is available during each season. They feature not only the cheeses that are at their height of flavour and production but also those that were made in the previous season and are now matured to perfection to be enjoyed.

Spring

△ **Valençay:** a soft goat's milk cheese in season in spring, summer and autumn when goats have given birth and produce fresh milk. Minimum maturation is four to five weeks, so the first artisan Valençay of the season is available in April. Valençay is an example of a whole family of young goat's milk cheeses that are spectacular come spring. Other examples are Chabichou du Poitou, Ste-Maure-de-Touraine, Pouligny-St-Pierre and Crottin de Chavignol.

△ **Appenzeller Extra:** a classic mountain cheese from Switzerland with a gorgeous smooth and rich texture. There are three main varieties on the market: Classic (silver label) – three to four months old; Surchoix (gold label) – four to six months old; and Extra (black label) – six months old plus. Only the best wheels get to become 'Extra'. It is made with early autumn milk and therefore is incredibly flavoursome come spring.

△ **Manchego Curado (nine months):** firm ewe's milk cheese that is synonymous with Spanish cheesemaking. Due to its popularity and mass appeal, it is available year-round if produced industrially. The best versions are artisan, especially if enjoyed extra mature. The cheeses produced during the height of summer when ewes are on grass will be ready to enjoy at the earliest the following spring.

△ **Gorgonzola Piccante:** this cheese is the lesser-known relation of the famous Gorgonzola Dolce but it is the original, whereas the milder Dolce version was invented much later to offer a wider appeal. This bold, spicy and firm blue cheese is matured for a minimum of six months, so if you enjoy it in spring you will be tasting the complex and luscious milk collected at the end of the summer/early autumn.

Summer

- △ **La Tur:** this gorgeously moussey cheese is available year-round but I especially love it in the summer. It's made from a blend of cow's, ewe's and goat's milk but the exact proportions of each will vary depending on the seasonal milk availability. In the summer, I find it offers the most complexity and it is as if someone turns the flavour intensity dial right up.

- △ **Comté (twenty-four months):** Comté is one of my most beloved cheeses but I particularly treasure the extra mature varieties. By law it's made only when cows are grazing on the green slopes of Jura but, by two years of age, the cheese starts to show its full flavour complexity and offers a nice crystally crunch.

- △ **Montgomery's Cheddar (twelve months):** an outstanding classic of British cheesemaking, Montgomery's cheddar is the industry standard for Somerset cheddar. I find it tastes best at about twelve months of age.

- △ **Cashel Blue:** this mellow but complex cow's milk blue is matured for a minimum of three months. I recommend tasting it in the summer and autumn. Its golden paste is lusciously dense and creamy, just the thing to enjoy with summer fruit and possibly cool ale.

- △ **Burrata:** not necessarily to go on a cheeseboard but a cheese that must be enjoyed in the summer, nonetheless. It is available throughout the year, in supermarkets as well as cheese shops, but the best burrata are made in the summer when cow's milk is fresh and is at its most flavoursome.

Autumn

△ **Baron Bigod:** this modern classic of British farmhouse cheesemaking is leading the way in the raw milk revival in the UK. It's a brie-style cheese made with raw Montbéliarde cow's milk and matured for a minimum of eight weeks. If you enjoy it in the autumn, you'll be savouring the essence of the land it comes from. In the summer, the cows graze on the rich variety of grasses and herbs that grow on Stow Fen, an unusual wildlife-rich basin marsh completely unique to the Waveney Valley in Suffolk.

△ **Sheep Rustler:** a winner of numerous awards and accolades, Sheep Rustler is another example of the outstanding artisan cheesemaking revival in Britain. Made in small (500 gram) wheels, this ewe's milk cheese tastes best at three months of maturation.

△ **Wyfe of Bath:** a stunning cow's milk gouda-style cheese from Somerset. It's made in an organic way and therefore it's got a real taste of place. The best examples are matured for a minimum of four months and are made with rich and wholesome summer milk.

△ **Biggar Blue:** one of the newest Scottish farmhouse cheeses, Biggar Blue is definitely worth a mention. Errington Cheese make it from their newly acquired herd of dairy goats and mature it for a minimum of two months.

Winter

△ **Rachel:** winter is not known to be the season for goat's milk cheese but Rachel solves this issue. It is a semi-firm gouda-style cheese that is normally matured for four to six months. That is why it offers an opportunity for goat's cheese lovers to enjoy it during the winter.

△ **Mimolette:** a striking and memorable Edam-style cheese that is scrumptious regardless of the season. If you can be patient and wait to enjoy it at eighteen months of maturity, you'll discover another dimension of complexity and even a lively crunch.

△ **Stichelton:** if you're born and bred in Britain, you know that the festive season is synonymous with Stilton. The reason for that is to do with the natural rhythms of life in the past. There was an abundance of milk in the summer, which was converted into large truckles of blue cheese that took five to six months to mature to their full potential. While Stilton is amazing, I personally have a soft spot for Stichelton, a raw milk version of Stilton. Raw milk is responsible for Stichelton's nuanced flavour and spectacular buttery texture.

△ **Vacherin Mont d'Or:** every cheese aficionado awaits the release of Vacherin Mont d'Or every year. This cheese is only made from 15 August until 15 March. With the minimum maturation requirement of twenty-one days, the first Vacherins are available in September, but I like to wait until the weather is much colder outside and enjoy it as a one-cheese fondue treat, which you can find in Chapter 7. It is the most soul-healing and heart-warming thing I can think of for long winter days.

The Ultimate Pasta Gratin

This recipe is also known in our house as 'fancy mac and cheese'. It serves four to six.

My family loves when I make this dish. The recipe has evolved over the years – starting as a classic mac and cheese with fine cheese, later enhanced with elements borrowed from a veggie bake and Tartiflette.

We don't have the Ultimate Pasta Gratin very often (it is rather rich), but when we do it is always a treat that we savour.

This recipe will seem like a lot of hard work, especially the first time you make it. It will also look like you've used every single saucepan and frying pan in the house. But it is worth the trouble! It is heart-warming, comforting and delicious, especially if you do not skimp on the quality of the cheeses used.

Take it slow the first time you make it, and if you can, enrol some help with boiling, chopping, grating, crumbling, and washing dishes. The crucial element of the dish is making the cheese sauce, so make sure to assign it to the most experienced cook, but the rest of the tasks can most certainly be delegated. Many hands make light work, but also think of this dish as an exercise in good communication and family bonding time. Have fun!

Ingredients

- 250-300g dry pasta (penne or fusilli)
- 500g broccoli and cauliflower
- 2 tbsp extra virgin olive oil
- 150g smoked lardons
- 2 shallots, chopped
- 100ml white wine
- 600ml of whole (or semi-skimmed) milk
- 30g butter
- 30g all-purpose flour
- 100g grated Parmigiano Reggiano (24 months)
- 150-200g grated Gruyère (12 months+)
- 0.5 tsp salt
- 0.25 tsp white pepper

Optional:

- △ 2 slices stale bread

- △ 2 sprigs thyme

- △ 20-30g flaked almonds

- △ Extra virgin olive oil

Method

1. Preheat the oven to 180°C/350°F.

2. Cook the pasta according to the directions on the pack. Drain, toss with some olive oil and set aside.

3. In a separate saucepan, boil medium-sized florets of cauliflower and broccoli for about 4-5 minutes (or until tender). When ready, add to the cooked pasta.

4. Meanwhile, heat a frying pan and fry the lardons and shallots for 4-5 minutes until golden-brown. Deglaze the pan with the white wine and continue to cook until most of the wine has evaporated. When ready, add to the pasta and veg mix.

5. Heat the milk (either on the stove or in the microwave). In another medium saucepan, melt the butter over medium heat until foamy. Remove from heat and whisk in the flour, stirring until a smooth roux has formed. Return the saucepan to medium heat, and begin to add the hot milk to the roux. You should add milk slowly, 100 ml at a time, completely

incorporating it before adding more (do not rush here as it's crucial for creating a smooth sauce).

6. After all the milk has been added, continue to whisk the sauce for another 2-3 minutes until it thickens. Then add the grated cheese (reserving some for the top), salt and pepper, and stir until the cheese has completely melted.

7. Pour the sauce over the pasta, lardon and veg mixture and then pour into a gratin dish.

8. Optional (but an absolute must for me): crumble the bread by hand (or blitz in a food processor), add thyme, almond flakes, some reserved cheese and olive oil. Mix it all together and scatter evenly over the pasta mixture.

9. Bake in the oven for 15-20 minutes (depending the strength of your oven) until golden and crunchy.

When it's ready, enjoy slowly and share with your favourite people.

Fine Cheese Vocabulary

Affinage: a French word for the process of maturing cheese, performed by a trained and knowledgeable professional (affineur), which helps each cheese to not only develop the expected flavour and texture but can also enhance its character beyond the standard expectation. Affinage is also known as cheese refinement. During maturation, the affineur will perform various activities with each cheese depending on the variety.

Affineur: a professional cheese maturer/refiner who understands the required treatment of each cheese according to its variety, monitors its development and performs maturation tasks, including flipping, washing, brushing, plucking and patting the cheese.

Artisan cheese: cheese made in a traditional way where the key stages of the process are performed by a professional cheesemaker, but the milk is sourced from nearby farms.

Bloomy rind: a type of skin on soft cheeses that is white in colour and mushroomy in aroma. It's predominantly made up of *penicillium candidum* and *geotrichum candidum* moulds. Typical for soft brie and camembert-style cheese.

Cheesemonger: a trained professional who has a full understanding of cheesemaking, styles and varieties, as well as matching cheese with other foods and beverages.

Cooked curd cheese: made when during the cheesemaking process its freshly made solids are heated to expel more whey. The resulting flavour of these cheeses is nutty, sweet and toasty. Classic examples are Comté, Gruyère and Parmigiano Reggiano.

Double crème: a variety of soft cheese that is enriched with cream during cheesemaking, raising its fat-in-dry-matter content to a minimum of 60% but not over 75%.

Farmhouse cheese: cheese made in a traditional way, in which the key stages of the process are performed by a professional cheesemaker, and is the product of one farm. That means that the milk for cheesemaking came from the same farm where the cheese was crafted.

Fine cheese: shorthand for farmhouse and artisan cheese.

Fromager: a French word for a professional cheesemonger (see above). Given France's gastronomic history, it is not surprising that this profession is held in much higher regard there than anywhere else in the world.

Pasteurised milk: milk that has been heated with the intention of killing pathogens that may be present. Pasteurisation of milk requires holding milk at temperatures of about 63°C for 30 minutes or over 72°C for 15 seconds. While it destroys potential pathogens, pasteurisation also kills off the 'good bacteria' that are ultimately responsible for creating flavour and character development in cheese.

Raw milk: milk straight from the animal without any heat treatment. Raw milk by nature contains a microcosm of bacteria. If treated properly, the good bacteria outnumber the bad and keep them in check. This type of milk will produce incredibly complex and wholesome cheese. If treated improperly, raw milk can potentially develop pathogens, so professional handling is essential.

Rennet: the substance used to separate curds and whey during cheesemaking. Rennet can be of animal, microbial or plant origin.

Maturation: see affinage.

Mountain cheese: cheeses produced in the mountainous regions of Europe, specifically the Alps and Pyrenees. They are typically made in large wheels and in a cooked curd style, then matured for extended periods of time of one year or more. The texture is usually smooth and sweet nutty notes prevail.

Natural rind: the type of rind on cheese that is essentially made of dried cheese and natural moulds present in the atmosphere during maturation. It is usually edible but may taste earthy.

Starter culture: the substance that kick-starts the cheesemaking process by converting milk sugars into lactic acid, creating a yoghurt-like texture. Starter cultures may be commercially made or natural.

Storage: the process of keeping the cheese after it has been cut.

Thermised milk: milk treated with heat to a temperature of between 57°C and 62°C for at least 15 seconds. It is a compromise between raw and pasteurised milk which makes it possible to destroy potential pathogens in the milk but not the flavour and character of the cheese.

Traditional cheesemaking: a labour-intensive process where the majority of work is performed and overseen by people with limited use of machinery. It is highly dependent on the quality of the raw material (milk), which will have seasonal and other effects on the process. An artisan cheesemaker knows the composition and seasonal variations of their milk so well that they know exactly what is required to turn it into a quality and characterful cheese.

Transhumance: migration of animals (usually cows and sheep) from the valley up to the mountains for the summer. They spend the summer grazing on the biologically pristine meadows, enjoying naturally organic grasses, herbs, flowers and water. For the winter, animals return to the valley and are put on dry feed until the next year.

Triple crème: a variety of soft cheese that is enriched with cream or crème fraîche during cheesemaking, raising its fat-in-dry-matter content to a minimum of 75%.

Vintage/Reserve: a term used when a particular fine cheese is matured for much longer than is standard for its variety.

Washed-curd cheese: cheese made by the process of removing some whey once it has separated from the curd and replacing it with water. As a result, the pH of the curd changes, creating a cheese that will be sweet and nutty in flavour. The most famous washed-curd cheese is Dutch gouda.

Washed rind: the type of rind that develops when cheeses are washed with a brine solution during maturation. The most prominent attributes of washed rind cheeses are their pungent/stinky aroma and bright orange colour of the rind.

Bibliography

Dunn, L, *Lagom: The Swedish art of balanced living* (Gaia, 2017)

Garcia, H, *Ikigai: The Japanese secret to a long and happy life* (Hutchinson, 2017)

Guiliano, M, *French Women Don't Get Fat: The Secret of Eating for Pleasure* (Vintage Books, 2006)

Kaufelt, R & Thorpe, L, *The Murray's Cheese Handbook: More Than 300 of the World's Best Cheeses* (Clarkson Potter, 2006)

Kindstedt, P, *American Farmstead Cheese: The Complete Guide to Making and Selling Artisan Cheeses* (Chelsea Green Publishing, 2005)

Kindstedt, P, *Cheese and Culture: A History of Cheese and its Place in Western Civilization* (Chelsea Green Publishing, 2012)

Luzzi, AF & James, WPT, 'European diet and public health: the continuing challenge', *Eurodiet* (2001)

McCalman, M & Gibbons, D, *Mastering Cheese: Lessons for Connoisseurship from a Maître Fromager* (Clarkson Potter, 2009)

Percival, B, *Reinventing the Wheel: Milk, Microbes and the Fight for Real Cheese* (Bloomsbury Sigma, 2017)

Shetty, J, *Think Like a Monk: The secret of how to harness the power of positivity and be happy now* (Thorsons, 2020)

Stuart, A, *Low Tox Life: A Handbook for a Healthy You and Happy Planet* (Murdoch Books, 2018)

Tunick, MH, *The Science of Cheese* (Oxford University Press, 2014)

Further Reading and Resources

Academy of Cheese: https://academyofcheese.org

Cheese in Pregnancy Blog: https://thecheeselady.co.uk/cheese-in-pregnancy

Cheeses from Switzerland: www.cheesesfromswitzerland.com/en/production/cheese-a-natural-product

Comté: www.comtecheese.co.uk

Eatwell Guide: www.nutrition.org.uk/healthyliving/healthydiet/eatwell.html

Fat: www.nhs.uk/live-well/eat-well/different-fats-nutrition

Fat: www.nutrition.org.uk/nutritionscience/nutrients-food-and-ingredients/fat.html?limitstart=0

Gruyère: www.gruyere.com

Health at a glance 2019: www.oecd.org/unitedkingdom/health-at-a-glance-uk-EN.pdf

Life expectancy: https://datacommons.org/ranking/LifeExpectancy_Person/Country

Mental Health Foundation, 'Food for thought: mental health and nutrition briefing' (2017): www.mentalhealth.org.uk/sites/default/files/food-for-thought-mental-health-nutrition-briefing-march-2017.pdf

Mental Health Foundation, 'Feeding minds: the impact of food on mental health' (2007): www.mentalhealth.org.uk/sites/default/files/Feeding-Minds.pdf

Mental Health Foundation, 'Stressed nation: 74% of UK "overwhelmed or unable to cope at some point in the past year"' (2018): www.mentalhealth.org.uk/news/stressed-nation-74-uk-overwhelmed-or-unable-cope-some-point-past-year

Mie, A et al., 'Human health implications of organic food and organic agriculture: a comprehensive review', *Environmental Health* (2017): www.ncbi.nlm.nih.gov/pmc/articles/PMC5658984

Acknowledgements

There are many people to whom I would like to acknowledge and express my deep gratitude.

My family - for believing in me and supporting me. You are my rock, my inspiration and my why. I feel blessed and thankful every day.

My customers - for your support, energy and constant inspiration. You make me want to be a better cheesemonger every day. It is my pleasure to be able to serve you.

My beta readers - Joy, Ken, Sheila and Evelyn - for your encouragement and constructive criticism that helped to improve this book tremendously.

All the cheesemakers mentioned in this book and beyond - for taking time out of their busy lives to show me around their farms and educate me on their cheese. My special thanks go to Humphrey Errington, Selina Cairns, Joe Schneider, everyone at the White Lake company and the Trethowan brothers.

My photographer - Amanda Farnese Heath - for her creativity, professionalism and enthusiasm.

My business friends Chet Morjaria, Jude Jennison and Rebecca Herbert - for keeping me accountable, as well as for supporting and inspiring me with your amazing achievements.

The team at Rethink Press - for your professionalism and dedication. You were a joy to work with.

The Author

Svetlana Kukharchuk is the founder of The Cheese Lady, based in Haddington, Scotland, and was previously the owner of The Guid Cheese Shop in St Andrews.

Svetlana has three university degrees in languages and international relations, but over fifteen years ago she gave up on a career in international politics to become a full-time cheesemonger at Murray's Cheese in New York City. Since then, she has travelled around the fine cheese world to learn from the best cheese retailers, traditional cheesemakers and maturers in the trade.

She has been a cheese judge at the Royal Highland Show and the World Cheese Awards, and holds a WSET Level 3 certificate, which qualifies her as a wine and spirits professional.

Svetlana's raison d'être is to champion farmhouse and artisan cheeses and to inspire joyful and mindful living. She wants to see a world where people enjoy natural foods in balance, with joy and in good company and as a result have lifelong wellbeing and strong social connections.

Svetlana and her family live in a beautiful coastal town in eastern Scotland.

🌐 www.thecheeselady.co.uk
f @TheCheeseLadyUK | ⊙ @TheCheeseLadyUK

Lightning Source UK Ltd.
Milton Keynes UK
UKHW020621130522
402934UK00005B/104